the
**WINEMAKER
COOKS**

the WINEMAKER COOKS

MENUS, PARTIES, AND PAIRINGS

CHRONICLE BOOKS
SAN FRANCISCO

by Christine Hanna

Photographs by Sheri Giblin

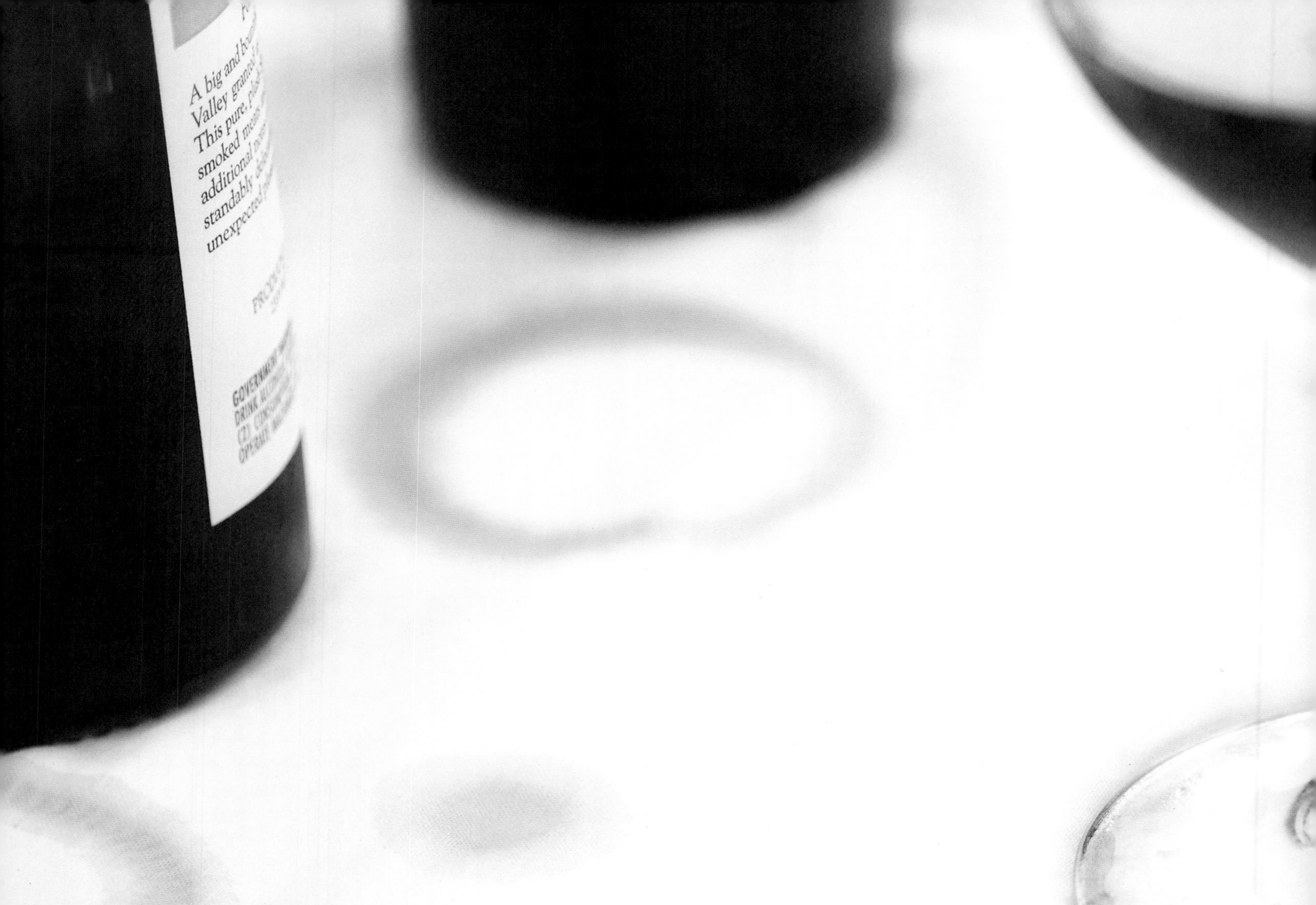

Text copyright © 2010 by Christine Hanna.
Photographs copyright © 2010 by Sheri Giblin.

Library of Congress Cataloging-in-Publication Data available.

ISBN 978-0-8118-6934-8

Manufactured in China

Designed by Brooke Johnson
Prop styling by Christine Wolheim
Food styling by Erin Quon
Typesetting by Janis Reed

10 9 8 7 6 5 4 3 2 1

Chronicle Books LLC
680 Second Street
San Francisco, California 94107
www.chroniclebooks.com

To Jake, for bringing the sunshine.
And to Abby and Brian, my favorite people to feed.

ACKNOWLEDGMENTS

This book would not be possible without the encouragement of Chronicle Books editor Bill LeBlond, who took a chance on this newbie author. Thank you for your creative input, your patience, and your advocacy. Thanks to the rest of the crackerjack team at Chronicle Books.

Thank you to Sheri Giblin for her extraordinary photography. She immediately fell in love with the project, and it shows. Thanks to Erin Quon for making the food look beautiful. There's no one I would rather cook with shoulder to shoulder. Thanks to Christine Wolheim for her beautiful props.

My father, Elias S. Hanna, MD made the vintner dream come true. Thanks to my sister Noel for the endless conversations that begin with, "Guess what I made for dinner last night?" Thanks to Honore and Chris, Mary and Dave, Sarah and Robert, and Kelley and Carlos for being appreciative and articulate critics during recipe testing. Thanks also for lending yourselves as subjects for the photography.

Thanks to the winemaking team at Hanna Winery, led by winemaker Jeff Hinchliffe. Your intelligence, humor, and curiosity are infectious.

Thanks to Randy for your writing encouragement and insider knowledge. Thanks to Liddi for knowing all the skeletons and still being there. Thanks to Anna for reattaching my body to my head!

Finally, thanks to Jake for his excellent editing skill, creative ideas, and cheerleading. You were right!

Contents

INTRODUCTION

Every Friday evening when I was a young girl, my parents loaded me, my four siblings, and the dog into our station wagon with the faux wood panels for the trek from our home in San Francisco to "the farm" in Sonoma County. My father had found twelve acres near Sebastopol, complete with cows, chickens, and an old barn, and it was there that we escaped our foggy weekday city life. On Saturday mornings, our first guests would arrive, families with children near our ages. I remember slicing home-grown tomatoes, making pesto, and marinating chicken with lemon and olive oil. There was plenty of wine for the grown-ups, and we kids forded the creek and chased the chickens around the property. Afternoons turned into evenings, and we all forged life-long friendships.

My father planted grapevines alongside the orchard and the vegetable garden, and we began to make our own wine, taking turns with the hand-cranked press and punching down the cap. A few years later, he hired a wine-maker and bought more acreage, and Hanna Winery was born. In the early nineties, I began to work full time at the winery, at first traveling the country to sell our wines, then gradually taking over the management of the business. Someone in the family needed to take a daily role, and my father was still a busy heart surgeon in San Francisco.

When I first moved to the wine country from the city, I was amazed at how the sidewalks rolled up in the evenings. After a 7 P.M. dinner reservation, there wasn't anything else to do. Cafes didn't stay open for an after-dinner espresso, there certainly weren't any nightclubs to dance away my dessert, and the latest movie screened at 8:30 P.M. What I soon learned was that wine country social life revolves around inviting people into your home. Dinner parties began with a glass of wine on the terrace overlooking the

setting sun on the grapevines. A leisurely dinner followed, stretching late into the evening with a final glass of wine around the fireplace, either indoors or out.

So I began to invite my new friends over for dinner. I started with my most comfortable menu repertoire, and took advantage of my lovely first house in Healdsburg, a Craftsman cottage with a huge backyard to make up for its diminutive rooms. Spring, summer, and fall, I'd set a table outside underneath a hundred-year-old Mission fig tree, and we'd watch the stars and enjoy our evening. Winter meals were more challenging, as only six could fit comfortably in the Douglas-fir-paneled dining room. However, it was at one of those very dinner parties that my husband-to-be and I first knew we would end up together, so sometimes small spaces make for the most intimate circumstances!

A year or so later, Jake and I moved from town to a country property in Alexander Valley, just minutes from Hanna Winery's second tasting room and vineyard. We now had two expanding wine clubs and a burgeoning visi-tor count, along with our wholesale accounts across the country. I wanted a peaceful place to come home to, with room to both relax and entertain. Our new home came with its own Cabernet vineyard, room for vast gar-dens, and plenty of space for indoor entertaining as well. Somehow, we were undaunted by the fact that the property and the house had been all but abandoned for decades, and that the plumbing, electrical, septic, and foundation all had to be redone. Talk about rose-colored glasses! But with two stone fireplaces, high ceilings, and lots of space, its charm and potential were undeni-able. I was sure we could return it to its former glory. We jumped in and began a multiyear process of restoring the old house, and did much of the work ourselves. We put together a makeshift kitchen first, of course. Not my dream kitchen by a long shot, but at least we had a place to cook and clean up in between work sessions.

Once the renovation dust had settled, I got back to cooking. My menus moved from standard repertoire to experimentation, using ingredients I'd pick up at the Saturday farmers' market. I started cooking like a California chef, organizing menus around what was freshest. And, I began to cook by looking through the vintner's lens, building menus around Hanna Winery's newest wine release. In the spring, the first of the vintage unoaked Sauvignon Blanc would take center stage, and the fava beans and ramps and young asparagus I found at the farmers' market just happened to pair beautifully. In the fall, when the nights got a little cooler, the fuller autumnal flavors of figs and butternut squash made fall-release reds like Zinfandel and Merlot sing.

Soon I was doing not just dinner parties, but Sunday brunches, summer pool parties with pizzas on the grill, elegant baby showers, and everything in between. And since I'm a busy working mother, I learned how to do them efficiently, with as much done ahead of time as possible so I could spend time with my guests and not be harried. As a guest, there's nothing more uncomfortable than feeling that your host is stressed out and overwhelmed.

I began to share my recipes with Hanna Winery's wine clubs and serve them at winery events. Soon, I had features in *Food & Wine*, *Savor*, and *In Wine Country*. I began to teach cooking classes that gave equal billing to wine pairing, and the idea for this book was born. My students were couples and singles who wanted to entertain with confidence and grace. Our three-hour classes flew

by, with lots of questions and laughter along the way. It occurred to me that wine country entertaining had more to do with a style of entertaining than simply a sense of place. Anyone, no matter where he or she lives, could entertain with seasonal ingredients, paired beautifully with wines.

In this book, I'll show you how to entertain wine country style, with its hallmark of casual elegance. The menus range from informal pizza parties to dinners worthy of entertaining your boss. The book is organized by season, and incorporates seasonal food ingredients as well as wines into each menu. Each section begins with what's ready to pick in the garden or is available at the local farm stand. You'll also get the inside scoop on seasonal activities in the vineyard, and what's being bottled and released in the cellar.

With wine as the centerpiece of seasonally focused entertaining. I take the mystery out of which wines to serve for which kinds of parties and why. Wines are chosen based on their compatibility with seasonal ingredients, the time of year, and the style of the event. A wintertime dinner party, for example, features rich and rustic Syrah to pair with the mushrooms and root vegetables so prevalent when the cold weather hits.

I answer the myriad of wine questions that I'm asked almost every day in my role as a vintner. These questions are highlighted in sidebars throughout the book, called "Ask the Winemaker." Corresponding to the menus and parties featured in that section of the book, they give answers to basic questions about making and serving wine.

Come join me on a trip to the lush landscape of Sonoma's wine country. I'll show you the insider view of wine country life, through the fields and vineyards of the valley, and into the cellar of Hanna Winery. We'll grab a basket and head to the farmers' market in our town of Healdsburg. We'll head home to the garden, to add fresh-picked produce to our bounty. And then we'll return to the kitchen to cook up seasonally inspired meals.

My Wine Country

The rhythm of the seasons begins with mustard blooming in the vineyard rows, the valley's first baby lambs with their wobbly legs, and farm stands filled with the ramps and baby artichokes of spring. The cellar wakes from its short winter nap. We begin to blend and bottle, releasing the first crisp whites of the vintage. Though the days may be warmer, the nights are tinged with frost, and the hum of the wind machines that warm the tender new grape shoots is audible throughout the valley.

By summer, the pace picks up. The voluptuous summer garden teems with cucumbers and zucchini, plums and peaches. We're racking, blending, and bottling to make room in the cellar for the new vintages of wine. We release our fuller-bodied oak-kissed white wines and our lighter reds. The vineyard is in full swing. We hear the clank and hum of tractors daily, and the hoots and hurrahs of singing vineyard crews as they make their way down a vine row to leaf, tuck, and tie.

In the fall, we bring in the grapes. And the tomatoes and melons and eggplants and figs. We see trucks stacked with grape bins making their way up and down our rural roads and two-lane highways. Wineries buzz late into the night. The farmers' markets are open several times a week now, with a dazzling array. We eat al fresco almost always, the grill replacing the range.

By October, the light turns golden, and the days are even warmer, though the nights are growing cooler. The cellar is full of newly pressed fermenting juice, the aroma drifting throughout the valley. Winemakers grab early-morning coffees with purple-stained hands, and the talk in town is of grapes, grapes, and more grapes. "How's your Chardonnay crop this year?" or "Are you all in yet?" Visitors flock to the tasting rooms to catch a glimpse of this magical time in wine country. And the leaves begin to turn golden to match the amber light of the afternoon and the straw-colored hills in the distance.

The race is on to finish harvest before the rains come in November. By then, the cellar will be full, and we'll press off daily, moving wines into fragrant new oak barrels. Nights are cold now, and sweaters are required during the day. And then the crowd of tourists thins, as people go home to join their families for Thanksgiving.

Our town feels emptier, but more neighborly. The farmers' market still groans with fall bounty, and we invite friends to join us for dinner as we move back inside. We light a fire in the living room and gather with a glass of red wine in hand, a braise gently simmering on the stove. The touch of frost brings us persimmons and pomegranates, cauliflower and winter greens. And we release the bolder red wines we want to drink when the temperature drops: Zinfandels and Merlots and Cabernets.

We open our homes for the holidays, inviting our wine country neighbors, who bring their own wares as gifts: homemade jams, breads, wines. The vineyard crews make their way slowly through the rows to prune before putting the vineyard to sleep for the winter.

This is the rhythm of wine country life.

Spring

Oh, spring! We all eagerly await the first blooms of impossibly yellow mustard flowers blooming between the vineyard rows, signaling warmer days ahead. We exult in the first bud break in the vineyard, tiny green leaves now adorning the bare, sculpted dormant vines of winter. The rains of winter subside and leave us with the fresh chartreuse of hillsides, the first sunny daffodils, and velvety purple iris. Our orchards bloom with the pink flowers of Santa Rosa plum and the coral ones of quince. We worry through the frosts of March and April, vineyard managers staying awake through the night to tend to their young, tender shoots. The first ramps and green garlic, baby artichokes and asparagus appear at the farmers' markets, and we start to think about entertaining outside again. The root vegetables and braises of winter give way to the delicate flavors and cooking techniques of spring. The lighter wines of spring accompany, with fresh and zingy Sauvignon Blanc and Pinot Gris taking center stage.

The Spring Garden

I love the spring garden, full of hope. I got married in the spring, so the celebratory spring meal is utter happiness to me. Citrus comes on strong through the early spring, Meyer lemon, blood orange, and lime giving us a bright zing after our long winter nap. The first asparagus poke out of the ground, to be paired with butter-napped morels, their earthiness a fleeting luxury. Artichokes are cradled within the spiky leaves of its plant. Shoots of green garlic, spring onions, and ramps push up from the moist spring soils. But the weeds! Along with the first green shoots and the tall fava beans that fall over to reveal pods ready to harvest come the spring weeds, which must be pulled before the seed pods break open and they take over our gardens! But we're so happy to be outside, on even a slightly warm day, that it feels good to tend the garden in earnest again. And finally, all that green gives way to crimson rhubarb and the very first strawberries, a taste of summer to come.

Springtime Lunch

○ ○ ○

Spring Salad of Favas and Manchego / 25

Farro with Sautéed Ramps and Asparagus / 26

Green Garlic–Marinated Flank Steak / 28

Tangelo-Honey Tart / 29

This lunch menu celebrates the gorgeous aromas of springtime. We move outside to a long table in the sunshine, with family-style platters of colorful spring salads, sautés, and the first grilled meats of the season. The table is set with lilacs, and the wine carries the fresh spring theme, with new-release unoaked Sauvignon Blanc from the cool Russian River Valley of Sonoma, its aromas of grapefruit and melon complementing the spring salad. A juicy Cabernet Franc would be perfect for the steak.

Spring Salad of Favas and Manchego || SERVES 6

We grow favas between the vineyard rows to fix nitrogen in the soil, with the added benefit of good eating! Fava beans are so easy to grow, and they come up like sentries in the springtime, with tall, leafy stalks and white flowers. They'll do wonders for your garden soil, too, without the need for chemical fertilizers.

This is a beautiful spring salad, all pale greens and whites. The chartreuse favas stand out like little jewels against the creamy color of Manchego curls. And after all, those bitter and leathery winter greens, it's lovely to have delicate lettuce again.

1 lb/455 g fava/broad beans in the pod

¼ cup/60 ml extra-virgin olive oil

1 tbsp sherry vinegar

1 tsp balsamic vinegar

½ tsp salt

¼ tsp freshly ground pepper

Leaves of 1 small head butter/Boston lettuce

4-oz/115-g piece Manchego cheese

Remove the beans from their pods. In a medium saucepan of boiling water, blanch the beans for 2 to 3 minutes. Drain and plunge into an ice bath. Pinch and remove the skins of the beans.

In a small bowl, combine the oil and the vinegars; whisk to blend. Whisk in the salt and pepper.

In a salad bowl, toss the lettuce leaves and beans with the vinaigrette and divide among 6 salad plates. Using a vegetable peeler, cut 3 to 4 thin curls of the cheese and place on each salad. Serve.

Farro with Sautéed Ramps and Asparagus ‖ SERVES 6

Farro has gained in popularity among the foodie crowd, and it's found more and more often on restaurant menus. An ancient Italian wheat similar to spelt, farro is wonderfully chewy and nutty when cooked, though it does require more cooking time than other grains.

Ramps, or wild onions, are a harbinger of spring; also known as wild leeks, they have a delicate flavor. They are often the first vegetables found in early-spring farmers' markets.

The first asparagus brings a glimmer of the warmer days ahead. Usually asparagus is a tough match for wine, but the nuttiness of the farro creates a bridge. The Sauvignon Blanc served with the salad is fine here, but the nutty farro allows for a low-tannin Cabernet Franc to pair nicely as well.

1 cup/170 g farro

2 tbsp salt

1 tbsp unsalted butter

2 tbsp extra-virgin olive oil

8 oz/225 g ramps, trimmed and cut into ½-in/12-mm diagonal pieces

1 lb/455 g asparagus, trimmed and cut into 1-in/2.5-cm diagonal pieces

½ tsp freshly ground pepper

Heat a large pot of water to boiling. Add the farro and 1 tbsp of the salt, cover, reduce heat to a simmer, and cook for 1 hour, or until the farro begins to pop open and tastes chewy. Drain and set aside.

In a large sauté pan, melt the butter with 1 tbsp of the olive oil over medium-high heat until the butter is foamy.

Add the ramps and asparagus, cover, and steam for 5 minutes, or until the asparagus is crisp-tender. Add the remaining salt and the pepper. Add the farro and toss gently to combine. Add the remaining 1 tbsp olive oil and toss to combine.

*What is the difference between
sparkling wine and Champagne?*

First, let's understand sparkling wine and Champagne's similarities. Both the terms *sparkling wine* and *Champagne* refer to wines containing large amounts of dissolved carbon dioxide gas that bubbles up and forms a lovely layer of foam on top of your flute glass. The most common method of making either sparkling wine or Champagne is to trap the gas produced when the wine goes through its second fermentation. Both sparkling wine and Champagne are made of either Chardonnay, Pinot Noir, and to a lesser extent, Pinot Meunier, or some combination. However, while sparkling wine refers to any wine with bubbles, Champagne's designation is much more exacting. To be labeled Champagne, the wine must be made in the Champagne region of France from grapes grown in that region, using the *methode champenoise*. In the *methode champenoise,* stainless-steel tanks or French oak barrels are used during the primary fermentation. The second fermentation, the one that results in all those lovely bubbles, occurs when sugar and yeast are added to the tank and the wine is bottled up. The wine is aged *sur lies*, on the yeast lees (lees are the deposits of residual yeast left at the bottom of a barrel or tank after fermentation). When wines are left to age on the lees, the wines develop a distinctive yeasty aroma and flavor. While still wines age on the lees in barrels or tanks, Champagne is bottled with the lees for a period of time. The yeast sediment is then disgorged. After disgorging, the dosage (a mixture of cane sugar, wine, and sometimes Cognac or brandy) is added to adjust the tartness in the wine. *Methode champenoise* requires a few months of bottle aging. Quality sparkling wine producers outside of France may also use the *methode champenoise,* but their wines cannot legally be called Champagne.

The French have fought long and hard to maintain this designation, much to the disappointment of California producers. Producers in very cool growing regions similar to the Champagne region of France, like the Russian River Valley of Sonoma County or the coastal regions of Mendocino, make sparkling wines that are excellent in quality. In fact, the French company Roederer makes a California sparkling wine from Mendocino using the same methods it uses to make its Champagne in France. Other sparkling wine alternatives from California and countries around the world, such as Italian Prosecco, Spanish Cava, Cremant from the Loire, and ruby-colored sparkling Shiraz, are generally simpler, less expensive wines not made using the *methode champenoise*.

Green Garlic–Marinated Flank Steak || SERVES 6

Green garlic is a delicate, adolescent version of the adult garlic bulbs you see in the grocery store. Found in the spring, it looks somewhat like a spring onion, but with that heavenly garlic scent and flavor instead. It's very easy to grow in your garden, and is usually one of the first things to poke through the earth when the soil warms up even a bit.

Serve a Cabernet Franc with this dish; more full bodied than a Pinot or a Merlot, it is still relatively low in tannins and has a subtle herbal quality that balances the berry flavors.

2 tbsp extra-virgin olive oil

¼ cup/60 ml Cabernet Franc or other light red wine

2 green garlic bulbs, trimmed and finely chopped

1 tsp salt

½ tsp freshly ground pepper

1½ lb/680 g flank steak

In a large, heavy self-sealing plastic bag, combine the oil, wine, green garlic, salt, and pepper. Add the flank steak. Close the bag and refrigerate for at least 2 hours or as long as overnight, turning the bag several times.

Heat a gas grill/barbecue to medium-high or prepare a medium-hot fire in a charcoal grill/barbecue. Shake off the excess marinade from the steak and grill for 5 to 7 minutes on each side for medium-rare. Transfer to a carving board and let rest for 10 minutes before cutting into thin diagonal slices.

Tangelo-Honey Tart || SERVES 6 TO 8

We're huge citrus fans in our family, despite the fact that I can't seem to grow it on our property. Those valley frosts really wreak havoc, though those who live in town have much better luck, as the temperature is just a bit warmer. A bike ride through the town of Healdsburg reveals ancient citrus trees on every block. Here, friends barter citrus for chicken eggs or wine, and everyone's happy.

Tangelos are a cross between tangerines and grapefruit or pomelos. They are very juicy, with little flesh. The sweetness of their tangerine flavor is tempered by the tanginess of the grapefruit, making for a sublime curd.

In this bright tart, tangelo curd is substituted for the more familiar lemon curd, and honey replaces some of the sugar. A classic short crust, almost cookie-like, is used. You can prepare both crust and curd a day ahead, making this tart perfect for a dinner party.

PASTRY DOUGH

1 cup/130 g all-purpose/plain flour

¼ tsp salt

½ cup/50 g confectioners'/icing sugar

6 tbsp/85 g cold unsalted butter, cut into chunks

1 large egg, beaten

FILLING

1 tbsp finely grated tangelo zest

⅔ cup/165 ml fresh tangelo juice

⅓ cup/75 ml fresh lime juice

¼ cup/60 ml honey

¼ cup/50 g granulated sugar

4 large eggs, beaten

Pinch of salt

½ cup/115 g plus 6 tbsp/85 g cold unsalted butter, cut into chunks

Tangelo segments and mint leaves for garnish

continued

For the dough: In a food processor, pulse the flour, salt, and confectioners'/icing sugar in a food processor until blended. Add the butter all at once and blend just until the mixture resembles pebbles. Add the egg and pulse until the mixture just begins to come together. It should not form a ball.

Turn the dough out onto a floured surface. Form into a ball and roll out into a 12-in/30.5-cm round. Transfer the dough to a 10-in/25-cm fluted tart pan/flan tin with removable bottom and fit the dough into the pan, pressing in against the sides. Run the rolling pin over the top of the pan to trim the top. Make sure the dough on the sides of the tart isn't too thin, as it will brown too quickly when baked. Wrap in plastic wrap and refrigerate for at least 2 hours or up to 2 days.

Adjust an oven rack in the center of the oven. Preheat the oven to 375°F/190°C/gas 5. Prick the bottom of the tart shell all over with the tines of a fork. Line the shell with parchment/baking paper and fill with dried beans or pie weights to keep the tart from shrinking and bubbling up while baking. Bake for 20 minutes, or until light golden brown.

Remove the beans or weights and the paper and continue baking for another 10 to 15 minutes, or until the shell is lightly golden. If the edges begin to brown too quickly, cover them with strips of foil so the base can brown as well. Transfer to a wire rack/cake cooler and let cool.

For the filling: In a medium saucepan, whisk together the zest, tangelo and lime juices, honey, sugar, eggs, and salt. Over medium-low heat, add the butter, a little at a time, whisking constantly until the curd is thick enough to coat the back of a spoon, about 10 minutes. Pour into the cooled tart shell and let cool.

Garnish with tangelo segments and mint. Remove the sides of the pan. Cut into wedges to serve.

How do I decipher a wine label?

Ah, the complexities of wine labeling. The Europeans label their wines based on geography. In France, for example, you'll see Burgundy, Bordeaux, or Champagne, but the grape variety will probably not be mentioned on either the front or the back label. If you shop by variety, you'll need to know that a red wine from Burgundy is bound to be made of Pinot Noir, and a Meursault from the same region is made of Chardonnay. In the United States, we label our wines based on grape variety, such as Pinot Noir, Cabernet Sauvignon, and Chardonnay. Seventy-five percent of the wine in the bottle must come from the variety specified on the label. The remaining 25 percent can be a mix of other varieties, or a single other variety. If a wine says "red table wine" or has a proprietary name like Joseph Phelps Insignia, that means that no single red variety makes up 75 percent of the blend, and the wine is instead made from some combination of lesser quantities of various varieties.

If a wine says "Estate Bottled" that means the winery must have grown 100 percent of the grapes used to make the wine at vineyards owned or controlled by the winery within their viticultural area. The winery must also have crushed, fermented, finished, and bottled the wine in a continuous process within that viticultural area.

The year on any wine label refers to the year in which the grapes for that wine were picked. The producer is usually most prominent on the label, and refers to the winery that made the wine. On California wine labels, you'll also find geographical information that tells you where a wine is made. On a bottle of Zinfandel, you might see Dry Creek Valley and Sonoma County. This tells you that the grapes for that Zinfandel were primarily sourced in the Dry Creek Valley of Sonoma County. On a bottle of Cabernet Sauvignon, you could see Napa Valley, which means the grapes were sourced anywhere in the Napa Valley, or you could see both Rutherford and Napa Valley on the label, which would tell you the grapes were sourced only from the Rutherford area of Napa Valley. You might see a vineyard name on the label as well, which further specifies the exact vineyard in which the grapes were grown.

Sometimes, you'll find the alcohol content on the front label, measured in a percentage. Usually it ranges from 13 to 15 percent. You might see the word *Reserve* on the label. This means different things to different wineries, and is unregulated in the United States. Generally, it means the best grapes or best lots from the best barrels at a winery. The back label can give you more information about the vineyard or winery, and may even discuss the blend or method of winemaking.

Spring Open House

○ ○ ○

Red Bliss Potatoes with Herbed Crème Fraîche / 34

Fava Bean Puree with Crudités and Crostini / 35

Lemongrass Tiger Prawns and Thai Noodle Salad / 37

Orange and Dijon–Marinated Pork Tenderloin / 38

Sugar Snap Peas and Spring Onions / 39

Strawberry Cardamom Shortcakes with Orange Blossom Cream / 40

I've served this menu for an elegant baby shower, as an alternative to the usual Easter ham, and as a springtime feast for my friends and neighbors. I greet my guests at the door with a festive glass of sparkling wine from Sonoma's Russian River Valley. Platters of hors d'oeuvres are plentiful, and a buffet celebrates the gorgeous colors of spring. We choose a crisp Sonoma Pinot Gris to match the aromatics of the prawn and noodle salad, and a light red like a Carneros Pinot Noir to pair with the delicate springtime flavors of the pork tenderloin.

The recipes serve 8 to 10 people, and can easily be multiplied to serve a crowd. It's a good idea to post a menu for a large party. Include not only the courses, but also the wines. Sometimes I've gone to a great party and been served a terrific wine, only to find the last empty bottle whisked away to an unattainable recycling bin before I can get a glimpse of the label or producer.

Red Bliss Potatoes with Herbed Crème Fraîche ‖ SERVES 8 TO 10

We grew potatoes for the first time last year. When the plants begin to flower, it's our cue to dig around in the soil beneath the plants to unearth the little potato gems, at least the ones without gopher nibbles. Sweet, fresh-dug homegrown potatoes are a revelation. If you don't grow your own, seek out spring, or new, potatoes, as they'll be sweeter than ones that have been overwintered.

This hors d'oeuvre couldn't be easier, and it looks beautiful on a platter. Any combination of delicate herbs will do for the crème fraîche. Sparkling wine is just the ticket to pair with the sweetness of the potatoes and the richness of crème fraîche.

16 small Red Bliss potatoes (about 2 in/5 cm in diameter), halved

½ cup/120 ml crème fraîche

2 tbsp finely chopped mixed fresh herbs, such as flat-leaf parsley, chives, and mint

Salt and freshly ground pepper

Fresh chives cut into 2-in/5-cm pieces for garnish

In a covered steamer over simmering water, cook the potatoes just until tender, about 10 minutes. Drain, rinse under cold water, and let cool completely.

In a small bowl, combine the crème fraîche and herbs and whisk to blend. Whisk in salt and pepper to taste.

Place the potato halves on a platter and dollop each with ½ tsp of the herbed crème fraîche. Lay a piece of chive on top of each potato half.

Fava Bean Puree with Crudités and Crostini | SERVES 8 TO 10

Here are our favorite springtime favas again, this time in a gorgeous puree. Small favas work best for salads and pastas, but the bigger, more starchy ones are just fine for this puree. Use the best extra-virgin olive oil you have for this recipe. It really makes a difference. The lush flavor of Pinot Gris will match the richness of the favas.

1½ lb/675 g fava/broad beans in the pod

1 tsp fresh lemon juice

1 small garlic clove, finely chopped

4 tbsp extra-virgin olive oil

½ tsp salt

¼ tsp freshly ground pepper

1 tsp finely chopped fresh mint

20 diagonal baguette slices, each ½ in/12 mm thick

Crudités for serving: sliced fennel, sliced celery hearts, and radishes

Remove the beans from their pods. In a medium saucepan of boiling water, blanch the beans for 2 to 3 minutes. Drain and plunge into an ice bath. Pinch and remove the skins of the beans.

In a food processor, puree the beans, lemon juice, and garlic until smooth. With the machine running, drizzle in 2 tbsp of the olive oil until emulsified. Add the salt, pepper, and mint and blend until incorporated.

Preheat the oven to 350°F/180°C/gas 4. Arrange the baguette slices in a single layer on a baking sheet/tray. Brush lightly with the remaining 2 tbsp olive oil. Bake until light golden brown, about 10 minutes. Don't let brown, as they should not be completely crisp through the center. Transfer to wire racks/cake coolers to cool. Serve the puree in a beautiful bowl, with the crostini and crudités alongside.

Lemongrass Tiger Prawns and Thai Noodle Salad || SERVES 8 TO 10

This Thai-inspired dish is another example of a do-ahead dish that tastes great at room temperature, making your job as cook and hostess all that much easier by avoiding any last-minute fuss in the kitchen.

The Thai flavors in this salad really make it stand out. We grow a kaffir lime just for the leaves and use it for any Thai flavoring. If you can't find the leaves in the market, you can substitute some lime zest. The lemongrass imparts a glorious aroma and flavor.

The bright acidity of Pinot Gris works beautifully with the zingy citrus and herb flavors in the salad.

2 stalks lemongrass, white parts only

Juice of 1 lime

1 tbsp grated peeled fresh ginger

1 tsp Asian sesame oil

2 tbsp extra-virgin olive oil

2 garlic cloves, finely chopped

1 fresh kaffir lime leaf, finely chopped

1 tsp salt

½ tsp freshly ground pepper

2 lb/910 g large tiger prawns, peeled and deveined

One 8-oz/225-g package bean thread noodles

DRESSING

2 tbsp rice wine vinegar

Juice of 1 lime

1 tsp Asian sesame oil

2 tbsp extra-virgin olive oil

1 tbsp finely chopped peeled fresh ginger

2 tsp soy sauce

½ tsp red pepper flakes

2 tbsp chopped fresh cilantro/fresh coriander, plus sprigs for garnish

2 tbsp finely chopped fresh mint

4 spring onions, finely chopped

Peel the outer layer of the lemongrass, then bruise the lemongrass with the heel of your knife to release the aroma. Cut the lemongrass into very fine crosswise slices and transfer to a large bowl.

Add the lime juice, ginger, sesame oil, olive oil, garlic, kaffir lime leaf, salt, and pepper to the bowl with the lemongrass. Add the prawns and toss to coat. Cover and refrigerate for 1 hour.

In a large sauté pan over medium-high heat, sauté the marinated prawns for 2 minutes on each side, or until just evenly pink. Do not crowd the pan. If you need to, work in batches. Transfer to a plate and let cool.

Meanwhile, put the noodles in a bowl and pour over boiling water to cover. Let stand for 5 minutes, then drain and set aside.

For the dressing: In a large bowl, whisk all the ingredients together.

Add the noodles and toss to combine. Add the prawns, chopped cilantro/fresh coriander, mint, and spring onions and toss to combine. Garnish with cilantro/fresh coriander sprigs.

Orange and Dijon-Marinated Pork Tenderloin ‖ SERVES 8 TO 10

We buy a pig at the Future Farmers Fair auction every year, which leaves us with a lot of pork in the freezer. In winter, I love to braise pork shoulder, and summer calls out for ribs, but spring seems destined for the more delicate and refined pork tenderloin.

Pork tenderloin marinates and grills quickly, and slices beautifully. It tastes terrific at room temperature, which makes it great for parties. Just don't overcook it. Better to pull it off the grill a bit underdone. It will continue to cook as it rests.

This is a great example of a dish that works with both white and red wine. The citrus flavors and bright acidity of Pinot Gris are a good match for the orange and Dijon flavors of the pork. The Carneros Pinot Noir has enough acidity to work with the marinade as well, and is a natural match with the tender pork medallions.

4 garlic cloves, finely chopped

2 tbsp Dijon mustard

2 tsp grated orange zest

Juice of 1 orange

2 tbsp extra-virgin olive oil

2 tsp salt

½ tsp freshly ground pepper

2 pork tenderloins

¼ cup/60 ml dry white wine

Two hours before you plan to grill the pork, combine the garlic, Dijon, orange zest and juice, olive oil, salt, and pepper in a large, self-sealing plastic bag. Add the pork tenderloins, turn to coat, close the bag, and refrigerate.

Remove the pork from the refrigerator 1 hour before cooking; remove from the bag, reserving the marinade. Preheat a gas grill/barbecue to medium-high, or prepare a medium-hot fire in a charcoal grill/barbecue. Grill the pork for 3 minutes on all sides. Transfer to a carving board, tent with aluminum foil, and let rest for 10 to 15 minutes.

Meanwhile, in a small saucepan, bring the marinade to a boil, add the wine, lower the heat to a simmer, and cook for about 5 minutes to reduce to a syrup.

Cut the pork into thin slices and serve with the warm syrup drizzled over it.

Sugar Snap Peas and Spring Onions || SERVES 8 TO 10

Fresh sugar snap peas are so good that they rarely even make it home from the farmers' market. My kids think they're as good as candy. This side dish pairs the crisp sweetness of sugar snap peas with spring onions. If you're convinced you have a black thumb, try growing spring onions. Gophers hate them, so do deer and most insects, and they sprout up like champs, even through many a frosty morning. They're so sweet you can eat them raw, but in this recipe they are sautéed with sugar snap peas, which makes the dish more wine friendly.

2 lb/455 g sugar snap peas

2 tbsp extra-virgin olive oil

4 spring onions, cut into ½-in/12-mm lengths

1 tsp salt

½ tsp freshly ground pepper

Snap off the stem end of each pea and pull off the string. In a large sauté pan, heat the olive oil over medium heat until shimmering. Add the onions and sauté for 1 minute.

Add the peas, salt, and pepper. Reduce the heat to medium-low, cover, and cook for 5 minutes, or until the peas are crisp-tender.

Strawberry Cardamom Shortcakes with Orange Blossom Cream || SERVES 6

We travel to the Eastern Mediterranean in this recipe, with aromatic cardamom in the shortcakes and orange-flower water flavoring the whipped cream.

The riper the strawberries, the less sugar you'll need, so the dessert wine on its own may make the strawberries taste perfect. Serve with a liqueur glass of the wine.

SHORTCAKES

2 cups/255 g all-purpose/plain flour

1 tbsp baking powder

½ tsp salt

1 tsp ground cardamom

3 tbsp sugar, plus 2 tsp

½ cup/115 g cold unsalted butter, cut into chunks

1 large egg

½ cup/120 ml half-and-half/half cream

1 large egg white, lightly beaten

STRAWBERRIES

4 cups/450 g fresh strawberries, quartered

¼ cup/60 ml dessert wine, such as Sauternes or late-harvest Sauvignon Blanc

Sugar as needed (optional)

ORANGE BLOSSOM CREAM

1 cup/240 ml heavy/double cream, chilled

1 tbsp sugar

1 tsp orange-flower water

For the shortcakes: Adjust an oven rack in the center of the oven. Preheat the oven to 425°F/220°C/gas 7.

In a food processor, pulse the flour, baking powder, salt, cardamom, and the 3 tbsp sugar together. Add the butter and pulse until the mixture resembles sand with small pebbles.

In a small bowl, whisk the egg and half-and-half/half cream together. Add to the food processor and pulse just until combined.

Turn the dough out onto a lightly floured surface and knead until combined. Lightly roll the dough out into an 8-in/20-cm round. Cut out 6 rounds with a 3-in/7.5-cm biscuit cutter.

Place the rounds on a baking sheet/tray and brush the tops with the egg white. Sprinkle with the 2 tsp sugar. Bake until golden brown, 12 to 14 minutes. Transfer the biscuits to a wire rack/cake cooler and let cool.

Meanwhile, for the strawberries: In a medium bowl, combine the strawberries and wine and macerate for 30 minutes. Taste and add sugar if needed.

For the cream: Using an electric mixer, beat the cream with the sugar and orange-flower water until soft peaks form.

To serve, cut the shortcakes in half and place the bottom half, cut side up, on a plate or platter. Top with some of the strawberry mixture and whipped cream, and place the top half of the shortcake on the top at an angle.

Springtime Brunch

∘ ∘ ∘

Artichoke, Prosciutto, and Chive Frittata / 45

Steelhead Trout with Leeks and Mustard Cream / 46

Minted Fresh Peas / 48

Warm New Potato Salad with Asparagus and Fresh Tarragon / 50

Meyer Lemon Tea Cake with Sauternes Glaze / 52

Our chickens are prolific in the springtime. Once the weather begins to warm, they each lay an egg daily, and this menu makes good use of their rich golden yolks. This springtime brunch is ideal for Mother's Day or Easter. The rich flavors of eggs and cream pair with a lush Sonoma or Napa Chardonnay. Artichokes can often be wine killers, but combined in the frittata with wine-friendly prosciutto and eggs, they work just fine in this menu. You can serve the cake with the same Sauternes to echo the flavor.

Artichoke, Prosciutto, and Chive Frittata || SERVES 6

Artichokes grow beautifully in all Mediterranean climates, including that of coastal California. Their foliage is sculptural and a beautiful silvery green, and their stalks are topped with tight-leaved globes. If you let an artichoke flower, you'll get a huge purple spiky mop-head that's just gorgeous in a modern flower arrangement. But we like to eat them too much to let them flower!

Normally, artichokes are a tough wine match, but the richness of eggs and prosciutto make this dish work. A lemony Sonoma Chardonnay is a perfect pairing here. Just make sure it's not too oaky.

---

3 globe artichokes

6 paper-thin slices prosciutto, finely chopped

2 small shallots, finely chopped

8 large eggs, beaten

¼ cup/60 ml half-and-half/half cream

¼ cup/30 g grated Parmesan cheese

1 tbsp finely chopped fresh chives

½ tsp salt

¼ tsp freshly ground pepper

Preheat the oven to 350°F/180°C/gas 4.

To trim the artichokes, pull off the tough outer leaves at the base. Cut off the top third of the artichoke crosswise, and continue trimming the leaves away until just the heart remains. Cut off all but 1 in/2.5 cm of the stem. Scoop out the choke with a spoon. Cut the artichoke hearts into 1-in/2.5-cm pieces. Set aside.

In a large ovenproof sauté pan, sauté the prosciutto and shallots over medium heat until the fat is rendered and the shallots are translucent, about 5 minutes. Add the artichoke hearts and sauté until heated through, 3 to 5 minutes.

Combine the eggs, half-and-half/half cream, Parmesan, chives, salt, and pepper and whisk to blend. Pour over the prosciutto, shallots, and artichokes in the pan. Cover, transfer to the oven, and bake for 15 to 20 minutes, or until the eggs are just cooked through. Run a spatula around the edge of the frittata to loosen. Invert onto a warmed plate and cut into wedges to serve.

Steelhead Trout with Leeks and Mustard Cream || SERVES 6

My dear friend Hunt Conrad is the author of the fishing column in the Healdsburg *Tribune*. Part information, part soapbox, Hunt's column chronicles his activities as an avid angler, not only here in Sonoma County, but up and down the West Coast. Early spring is the tail end of steelhead season, and Hunt can be counted on for fresh catch from the Russian River. There is nothing like the taste and texture of fish caught just hours before. My job is to come up with a recipe to match the freshness of the fish.

Steelhead are trout that act like salmon. Born in small streams, they migrate to the sea for most of their adult life, then return to the streams to spawn. Steelhead is often mistaken for salmon because of its beautiful peach-colored flesh. Ask your fishmonger to debone the fish for you. If you can't find steelhead, feel free to substitute wild salmon for this recipe.

Chardonnay's natural acidity cuts through the richness of the mustard cream sauce beautifully here.

Six 4-oz/115-g steelhead or salmon fillets

1 tsp salt

½ tsp freshly ground pepper

2 tbsp unsalted butter

½ cup/60 ml dry white wine

2 leeks, white parts only, finely chopped

¼ cup/60 ml heavy/double cream

1 tbsp Dijon mustard

Liberally season the fish on both sides with salt and pepper. In a large frying pan, melt the butter over medium heat until it is foaming. Add the fish and sauté for 2 minutes on each side. Transfer to a warm plate. Reduce heat to medium-low, add the wine and leeks, and sauté until the leeks are soft, about 5 minutes. Stir in the cream and mustard. Add the fish to the pan, baste with the sauce, cover, and cook over medium-low heat until still translucent in the center, about 5 minutes. The fish will continue to cook through off heat. Serve topped with sauce.

Minted Fresh Peas || SERVES 6

When fresh peas are in the market in early spring, it's cause for celebration. But they must be fresh. A starchy pea is no good at all, and you may as well buy them frozen. Choose bright green peas with squeaky, firm pods. Do not buy them if they're yellowed or wilted. All these delicious peas need is a quick sauté in butter and a little fresh mint, salt, and pepper. Even if you only have a pot on a terrace, try growing some fresh mint for dishes like these, and for fresh mint tea.

2 tbsp unsalted butter

1½ lb/680 g green peas in the pods, shucked

2 tbsp finely chopped fresh mint

Salt and freshly ground pepper

Melt the butter over medium heat in a medium sauté pan until just foaming. Add the peas and sauté for 2 to 3 minutes, or until just cooked through but not soft. Stir in the mint and salt and pepper to taste. Serve at once.

ASK THE WINEMAKER

What is an appellation?

An appellation is a geographical area where grapes are grown and wines are produced. The rules governing appellation designations depend on the country the wine is produced in. In the United States, appellations are county names, such as Sonoma County, which is one of the largest producers of wine grapes in the country. Within the Sonoma County appellation, there are thirteen American Viticultural Areas, or AVAs, such as Dry Creek Valley, Russian River Valley, and Alexander Valley. An AVA is a geographical area that has a distinctive climate, kind of soil, elevation, and physical features. Napa County is an appellation as well as an AVA, as are AVAs within Napa Valley, like Oakville and Rutherford. If an AVA is stipulated on a wine bottle, 85 percent of the grapes in that wine must be from that specific AVA.

An appellation gives you a reference point for understanding a wine. A sense of place, or *terroir*, is crucial for quality wines, a philosophy that European winemakers have followed for centuries.

Warm New Potato Salad with Asparagus and Fresh Tarragon || SERVES 6

Here are our lovely homegrown new potatoes again, this time in a warm spring salad. Use small new potatoes for this salad, along with spring's first tender asparagus. The salad is napped with extra-virgin olive oil, a little vinegar, and fresh tarragon, rather than a cloying mayonnaise. You can serve it at room temperature, but it's best warm. If you don't have room for a garden, try growing fresh herbs in a pot on your windowsill. Fresh tarragon makes all the difference in this recipe.

18 to 20 small new potatoes, whole or halved

1 tbsp extra-virgin olive oil, plus ¼ cup/60 ml

2 shallots, finely chopped

1 lb/455 g asparagus, trimmed and cut into 2-in/12-mm diagonal pieces

1 tsp salt

½ tsp freshly ground pepper

1 tbsp sherry vinegar

1 tbsp finely chopped fresh tarragon

In a covered steamer over simmering water, cook the potatoes for 10 to 15 minutes, or just until tender.

Meanwhile, in a medium sauté pan, heat the 1 tbsp olive oil over medium heat just until shimmering. Add the shallots and sauté until translucent, about 3 minutes. Add the asparagus, salt, and pepper. Cover and cook for 2 to 3 minutes, or until crisp-tender.

Drain the potatoes and transfer to a large bowl. Add the asparagus mixture, then the ¼ cup/60 ml olive oil, the vinegar, and tarragon. Toss to combine. Taste and adjust the seasoning and serve at once.

Meyer Lemon Tea Cake with Sauternes Glaze || SERVES 8 TO 10

Meyer lemons are like gold around here! I look forward to their fragrant tangerine aroma and juice all year. They first begin to ripen in late winter into early spring. Those lucky enough to have a Meyer lemon tree in their backyard are in for some excellent bartering. Citrus doesn't do very well on my property, so each year I happily trade bottles of our Sauvignon Blanc for bagfuls of Meyer lemons. Once home, I arrange them in a bowl on the kitchen table, where they release their heady fragrance throughout the house.

This fragrant Meyer lemon tea cake is spiked with a glaze of dessert wine and sugar, a perfect ending to a springtime brunch. You may double the recipe and bake it in a Bundt pan if you wish. Just remember to double the glaze as well.

Serve this cake with the same Sauternes you use in the glaze.

CAKE

1½ cups/195 g all-purpose/plain flour

¼ tsp baking powder

¼ tsp baking soda/bicarbonate of soda

½ tsp salt

½ cup/115 g unsalted butter at room temperature

1 cup/200 g sugar

2 large eggs at room temperature

Grated zest of 2 Meyer lemons

2 tbsp fresh Meyer lemon juice

½ cup/120 ml buttermilk

½ tsp vanilla extract/essence

GLAZE

½ cup/120 ml Sauternes or other white dessert wine

½ cup/100 g sugar

1 tsp grated Meyer lemon zest

For the cake: Adjust an oven rack in the center of the oven. Preheat the oven to 350°F/180°C/gas 4. Butter and flour a 9-by-4-in/23-by-10-cm loaf pan/tin; knock out the excess flour.

Sift the flour, baking powder, baking soda/bicarbonate of soda, and salt together into a medium bowl. Set aside.

Using a stand mixer fitted with a paddle attachment, cream the butter and sugar until fluffy, about 5 minutes, stopping once or twice to scrape down the sides of the bowl. Add the eggs, one at a time, scraping down the sides of the bowl as needed. Add the lemon zest, lemon juice, buttermilk, and vanilla and beat to combine.

Add half of the flour mixture to the bowl and mix until just incorporated. Add the remaining flour mixture and mix until just combined; scrape down the sides of the bowl as needed.

Pour the batter into the prepared pan and smooth the top with a spatula. Bake for 55 minutes, or until a tester inserted in the center comes out clean. Let cool for 10 minutes. Run a knife around the edge of the cake and unmold onto a wire rack/cake cooler. Set the cake right side up on the rack with a baking sheet/tray underneath.

For the glaze: In a small saucepan, combine the wine, sugar, and lemon zest. Bring to a boil over high heat, then reduce heat to medium-low. Cook for about 10 minutes, until the sugar is dissolved and the mixture is thickened.

While the cake is still warm and on its rack/cake cooler, poke deep holes through the cake with a wooden skewer. Pour the glaze over the cake. Let cool. Slice and serve.

ASK THE WINEMAKER

How do wines get their color?

Wines get their color from the skins of the grapes used to make them. White wines made with white grapes range from a pale straw color to a more golden hue. Red wines made with red grapes are a deep purple color. However, you can make white wine from red grapes if the skins are immediately removed from the crushed juice. If the skins are left in a little longer, a blush color results. Rosé Champagne uses this method to coax a lovely peachy rose color from Pinot Noir grapes. Still rosé wines are generally made from Syrah, Grenache, and Merlot grapes that are left on the skins a very short time.

Impressive Spring Dinner

○ ○ ○

Caviar with Crème Fraîche on Brioche Toast / 56

Cream of Sorrel Soup / 58

Yukon Gold and Melted Leek Gratin / 59

Herbed Lamb Roulade with Merlot Jus / 60

Rhubarb Pots de Crème / 62

The first time I cooked a major dinner at home for business associates, I was scared out of my wits. But once I understood how appreciative guests are to be invited into your home, I relaxed and had fun with it. This is a pull-out-the-stops dinner good enough for your boss or your best friends.

For small dinner parties, I like to serve a variety of wines. A brut or rosé Champagne is a festive and luxurious way to start. A Riesling from Mendocino, Sonoma, or Napa would be ideal with the lemony sorrel soup, and a fuller-bodied Alexander Valley Merlot is just right with the lamb. A Moscato, with its touch of sweet effervescence, is a lovely companion for the pots de crème.

Caviar with Crème Fraîche on Brioche Toast || SERVES 6

Cyrus, a wonderful and luxurious restaurant in Healdsburg, serves a caviar and Champagne course to set the tone for the meal to come. Here is my own version for special-occasion dinners.

California produces white sturgeon caviar that's worthy of a formal meal and costs significantly less than the imported version. You can substitute salmon roe if you prefer. The buttery, slightly sweet brioche toast is a nice foil to the tangy crème fraîche and salty caviar.

Serve a brut Champagne with this appetizer.

Six to eight ½-in-/12-mm-thick brioche slices, crusts removed

½ cup/120 ml crème fraîche

1 oz/30 g caviar

Lightly toast the brioche slices. Using a metal ring or a small glass, cut the toasts into eighteen rounds 2 to 3 in/ 5 to 7.5 cm in diameter. Top each round with ½ tsp crème fraîche and ¼ tsp caviar.

ASK THE WINEMAKER

How do I know how much wine to buy for a party?

The general rule of thumb is that one bottle yields five glasses. For a dinner party for eight, I usually plan on two bottles of white wine or Champagne to start. Then, once we sit, I plan on two bottles of each wine for each course. Double up if you're serving the same wine for two courses.

For an open house or a big party of about thirty people, figure on eight bottles of white and eight bottles of red. That way, everyone gets at least two glasses, with some left over. Do pay some attention to the weather. In the summer, especially if you're entertaining outdoors, you will go through more white wine than red. In the winter, you'll go through more red than white.

Cream of Sorrel Soup

Sorrel has broad, sword-like bright green leaves and grows like a weed in my garden almost year-round, but is especially prolific in the spring after its winter nap. You'll start to see it at farmers' markets shortly after the last frost. It's used as an addition to fresh salads, but I love it in this lemony soup. The only downside is that sorrel turns army green in color when cooked, but since this is a dinner party, in the candlelight it will look lovely nonetheless. Garnish with a little extra cream and fresh parsley and no one will notice.

Pour a bright, aromatic Riesling with the soup. The acidity will be a nice match with the sorrel. Alsace sets the standard for Riesling, but producers from cool climates of California, Oregon, and Washington are catching up.

2 tbsp unsalted butter

1 onion, finely chopped

1 large Yukon Gold potato, peeled and diced

2 cups/480 ml chicken stock

1 lb/455 g sorrel, stemmed and coarsely chopped

½ cup/120 ml heavy/double cream, plus extra for garnish

1 tsp salt

½ tsp freshly ground pepper

2 tbsp finely chopped fresh flat-leaf parsley for garnish

In a heavy soup pot, melt the butter over medium heat just until foaming. Reduce the heat to medium-low and sauté the onion until translucent, about 5 minutes. Add the potato and sauté for 2 to 3 minutes. Add the chicken stock and simmer for 15 minutes, or until the potato is very soft. Stir in the sorrel and remove from heat. Cover and let stand for 5 minutes, or until the sorrel is wilted.

In batches, puree the soup in a blender and return to the pot. Add the ½ cup/120 ml cream, the salt, and pepper. Ladle into bowls and garnish with extra cream and the parsley.

Yukon Gold and Melted Leek Gratin | SERVES 6

The beauty of this potato gratin is that absolutely everyone loves it. Serve a square under a slice of roast lamb drizzled with its juice and your guests will be transported. I've upgraded the standard potato gratin using buttery Yukon Golds and melted leeks along with a nutty Gruyère cheese.

2 tbsp unsalted butter

2 leeks, white and pale green parts only, cut into 1-in/2.5-cm cubes

6 large Yukon Gold potatoes, peeled and very thinly sliced

1½ cups/175 g shredded Gruyère cheese

Salt and and freshly ground pepper

1 cup/240 ml heavy/double cream

Preheat the oven to 350°F/180°C/gas 4. In a large sauté pan, melt the butter over medium heat just until foaming. Reduce heat to low and sauté the leeks until very soft, about 10 minutes.

In a large gratin dish, alternate layers of potatoes, leeks, and cheese, seasoning each layer with salt and pepper.

Finish with a final sprinkling of cheese. Pour the cream over the gratin. Cover lightly with aluminum foil and bake for 40 minutes. Uncover and bake for another 30 to 40 minutes, or until bubbling and brown on top. Let cool slightly. Cut into squares to serve.

Herbed Lamb Roulade with Merlot Jus ||

Along with a pig, we buy a lamb every year at auction. It's sweeter in taste than supermarket lamb, and even guests who don't usually like lamb are converted once they try this aromatic roast.

With its swirls of bright green herbs, the roulade is beautiful when sliced. The Merlot jus is a snap to make while the roast rests. Have your butcher butterfly the lamb to get it as uniformly flat as possible. You can even it out more by pounding once you get it home.

The Merlot is perfect with the lamb and herb flavors.

1 boned and butterflied leg of lamb, 3 to 4 lb/910 g to 1.4 kg

1 cup/30 g finely chopped mixed fresh herbs, such as oregano, sage, thyme, or rosemary

4 garlic cloves, finely chopped

2 tbsp extra-virgin olive oil

1 tbsp salt, plus more to finish

1 tsp ground black pepper, plus more to finish

½ cup/120 ml Merlot or other dry red wine

½ cup/120 ml best-quality lamb or beef stock

Pound the lamb with a mallet to uniform thickness. In a small bowl, combine the herbs, garlic, olive oil, salt, and pepper into a paste. Spread the paste evenly on top of the lamb. Starting from one end, roll the lamb up in a spiral. Tie the lamb together with kitchen twine. Let stand at room temperature for 1 to 2 hours.

Preheat the oven to 450°F/230°C/gas 8. Sprinkle the lamb with salt and pepper. Place in a roasting pan/tray on a rack and roast for 10 minutes. Turn the lamb over and roast for 10 minutes more. Reduce the oven temperature and roast for another 30 minutes for a total of 50 minutes,

or until an instant-read thermometer inserted in the center of the roulade registers 130°F/54°C for medium-rare. Transfer to a carving board, tent with aluminum foil, and let stand for 10 minutes.

Meanwhile, place the roasting pan/tray over medium heat. Add the Merlot and stock. Stir to scrape up the browned bits from the bottom of the pan and cook to reduce the liquid by half. Using a fine-mesh sieve, strain the jus into a bowl.

To serve, cut the lamb into slices and drizzle with the jus.

Rhubarb Pots de Crème ‖ SERVES 6

Don't you love rhubarb? Its fleeting season heralds springtime, but for this menu I wanted something a little more elegant than the usual rhubarb pies and tarts. Pots de crème are elegant little custards for a formal dinner party. In these, a layer of ruby red rhubarb compote is hidden under a velvety vanilla custard. They can be made a day or two ahead and kept chilled in the refrigerator for stress-free dinner-party dessert.

A slightly effervescent Moscato is a perfect companion.

1 lb/455 g rhubarb, cut crosswise
    into 1-in/2.5-cm pieces
1 cup/200 g sugar

1 cup/240 ml milk
1 cup/240 ml heavy/double cream

1 tsp vanilla extract/essence
4 large egg yolks
Pinch of salt

In a medium nonreactive saucepan, stir the rhubarb and ½ cup/100 g of the sugar together and let stand until the rhubarb begins to release its juices, about 10 minutes. Bring to a boil, reduce heat to a simmer, and cook for about 5 minutes, or until the rhubarb is completely soft and beginning to break down. Remove from heat and let cool completely.

Adjust an oven rack in the center of the oven. Preheat the oven to 325°F/165°C/gas 3. In a small saucepan, combine the milk, cream, and vanilla. Bring just to a simmer over medium heat. Turn off heat.

In a medium bowl, whisk together the egg yolks, the remaining ½ cup/100 g sugar, and the salt. Ladle one scoop of the warm cream mixture into the egg yolk mixture to temper. Whisk in the remaining cream mixture. If you have egg solids, then strain. If not, you may skip that step.

Arrange six 6-oz/170-g ovenproof ramekins in a roasting pan/tray with sides as high as the ramekins. Spoon enough rhubarb compote into each ramekin to measure one-fourth of the way up the side. Divide the custard among the ramekins, filling them no more than three-fourths full. Pour boiling water into the roasting pan/tray to reach halfway up the sides of the ramekins, making sure not to splash any into the custard. Cover the pan with aluminum foil and poke a few holes in the top so steam can escape.

Bake until the custards are set, about 30 minutes. Transfer the cups to a wire rack/cake cooler to cool completely. Cover the ramekins with plastic wrap and refrigerate until set, at least 2 hours or overnight. Serve chilled or at room temperature.

Variation: Sprinkle the top of each pot de crème with 1 tsp sugar and place under a broiler/grill for a few minutes until the top is browned. Serve warm or at room temperature.

What does it mean when a wine is "corked"?

A corked wine is a wine that has been contaminated by a flawed cork. A chemical compound called TCA, or trichloranisole, infects the cork with a mold that smells like musty, moldy cardboard. It ruins a wine, and unfortunately, many consumers don't know what it is and just think the producer made a bad wine. Many experts in the industry think that as much as 10 percent of wine can be flawed in this way. As a result, wineries are looking for alternative closures to the cork. Screw caps have become very popular, particularly with quick-to-market whites like Sauvignon Blanc. The main objection to the screw cap is we're not sure how wines age with this closure. There is some evidence that preventing any oxygen from entering the bottle (corks allow a bit of oxygen in to gracefully age the wine) inhibits the aging process and lessens a wine's aroma or flavor. Other closure options are synthetic corks made of plastic, glass stoppers, and composite corks made of a combination of cork and synthetic material.

I am a big fan of the screw top. I worry about glass chipping on the glass stoppers, so that doesn't work for me. Synthetic corks are made of plastic and are harder to get in and out of the bottle, and I think the plastic off-gasses and gives the wine a funny smell. I say, embrace the screw cap!

Weeknight Dinner

∘ ∘ ∘

Rosemary-Roasted Marcona Almonds / 65

Orrechiette Carbonara with Asparagus / 67

Shaved Fennel and Herb Salad with Baby Radishes / 68

Balsamic Strawberries with Honeyed Ricotta / 69

We all have those after-work/-school/-soccer weeknights when we get home late but still want to eat something delicious and homemade. This dinner comes together in a snap, and is elegant enough for an impromptu dinner party. A medium-acidity Chenin Blanc works nicely here with the asparagus. You may need to search for this wine, but a few producers, like my neighbor Leo Steen, are still making it. As for reds, think light Italian. A California Italian Sangiovese would be perfect with the pasta.

Rosemary-Roasted Marcona Almonds || MAKES 2 CUPS/230 G

I always have some version of these in the fridge for snacks. Marcona almonds are indigenous to the Mediterranean coast of Spain. Their shape is flatter than the typical almond, and their taste is sweeter and more delicate. If you don't have almonds, you can substitute walnuts or pecans. No rosemary? Try sage or oregano. A little bit of sugar brings out the sweetness in the almonds and is a nice foil for the herb. If you make these ahead of time, place them in a ramekin and warm slightly in the oven to serve.

2 cups/230 g Marcona almonds

2 tbsp unsalted butter, melted

1 tbsp finely chopped fresh rosemary

1 tsp sugar

1 tsp salt

½ tsp freshly ground pepper

Preheat the oven to 350°F/180°C/gas 4. Spread the almonds on a rimmed baking sheet/tray in a single layer. Toss with the melted butter, rosemary, sugar, salt, and pepper. Roast for 10 to 15 minutes, or until nicely browned (watch carefully, as nuts burn quite easily). Serve at room temperature or slightly warm.

Orrechiette Carbonara with Asparagus || SERVES 6

Pasta carbonara is the ultimate comfort food. Pasta, eggs, cheese, a little cream, and some kind of bacon is just heaven. To counteract the cholesterol hit, I add a green vegetable, in this case, spring asparagus. I like pancetta for carbonara because it's not as smoky-tasting as bacon, but you may substitute prosciutto or regular bacon if you wish.

Orrechiette is the pasta that looks like little ears, and kids just love them. They even gobble up the green stuff alongside. The only trick to making any kind of carbonara is getting the temperature right. If the eggs are too cold, they'll never cook through in the warmth of the pasta and you'll have to turn the burner on, inevitably creating scrambled eggs. So take your eggs, cheese, and cream out of the refrigerator for an hour or so before making this dish, and everything will cook through perfectly without any added heat. A Chenin Blanc has just enough acidity to cut through the richness of the pasta sauce. If you're hankering for a red, go for a Sangiovese from California or Italy.

---

6 oz/170 g pancetta, cut into small dice

2 shallots, finely chopped

¼ cup/60 ml dry white wine, such as Chenin Blanc or Pinot Grigio

8 spears asparagus, cut into 1-in/2.5-cm diagonal pieces

12 oz/340 g orrechiette pasta

3 large eggs at room temperature

¾ cup/90 g grated Parmigiano-Reggiano cheese

¼ cup/60 ml heavy/double cream at room temperature

½ tsp salt

½ tsp freshly ground pepper

In a large sauté pan or frying pan, sauté the pancetta over medium heat until it begins to render its fat, about 3 minutes. Add the shallots and sauté for about 10 minutes, or until the shallots are translucent and the pancetta has rendered its fat completely. Add the wine, scaping up any browned bits. Stir in the asparagus, cover, turn off heat to let the asparagus steam.

Meanwhile, in a large pot of salted boiling water, cook the pasta until al dente, about 10 minutes. In a medium bowl, whisk together the eggs, ½ cup/60 g of the cheese, the cream, salt, and pepper. Set aside.

Stir the drained pasta, then the egg mixture, into the pan with the warm asparagus. The heat of the pasta and the pan will cook the eggs.

Divide among warmed plates, garnish with the remaining ¼ cup/30 g cheese, and serve.

Shaved Fennel and Herb Salad with Baby Radishes || SERVES 6

The very best fennel comes up in the spring. By the time the hot weather hits, its fronds go to seed, and the bulbs, though bigger, aren't nearly as sweet. Fennel has a lovely anise flavor and a terrific crunch. A mandoline is an easy way to get uniform paper-thin fennel slices, but you can also use a sharp knife. Choose smaller bulbs rather than gargantuan ones. They'll be much less tough, and you won't have to toss the outer leaves.

Chenin Blanc's lemony acidity works nicely with the anise flavor of the salad.

1 small fennel bulb, trimmed, halved lengthwise, and cored

4 baby radishes, sliced thinly

2 handfuls spring lettuces or mixed baby greens

¼ cup/10 g finely chopped mixed fresh chives, flat-leaf parsley, and mint

¼ cup/60 g extra-virgin olive oil

2 tsp Champagne vinegar

½ tsp sea salt

¼ tsp freshly ground pepper

Thinly shave the fennel halves with a mandoline, or slice thinly crosswise.

In a medium salad bowl, combine the fennel, radishes, lettuces, and herbs. In a small bowl, whisk together the olive oil, vinegar, salt, and pepper. Add to the vegetables and toss to combine.

Balsamic Strawberries with Honeyed Ricotta ‖ SERVES 6

We grow strawberries in a raised bed right inside our garden gate. My son, Brian, scans the patch every day for the slightest hint of red ripened fruit. The ones he misses make it into this lovely dessert. Balsamic vinegar adds a touch of acid and sophistication to the macerated berries.

This is another quick and delicious dessert that's also very light. If you want to gild the lily and serve it with sugar cookies or shortbread, go right ahead. Fresh ricotta is the best option for this dish. Its texture is ethereal and its flavor slightly milky. You can find fresh ricotta at a cheese shop or at most specialty grocery stores. If you can't find fresh ricotta, use the supermarket variety, but add a little extra honey.

4 cups/455 g fresh strawberries, quartered

2 tbsp balsamic vinegar

2 tbsp sugar

2 cups/455 g fresh whole-milk ricotta cheese

2 tbsp honey

In a medium bowl, toss the strawberries with the vinegar and sugar and let stand for 20 minutes.

If the ricotta is very fresh, suspend it in a cheesecloth/muslin-lined sieve over a medium bowl for 10 minutes to remove excess liquid. Remove from the cheesecloth/muslin and transfer to a small bowl. Stir in the honey.

To serve, place a mound of honeyed ricotta onto each plate. Place some berries alongside, drizzling them with any remaining juices.

Summer

Summer in wine country is delicious indeed. Warm, sunny days stretch with no end in sight. The evenings bring cool breezes through screen doors and windows, fragrant with the day's sun-kissed golden grasses. We spend much of our time outside, beginning in the early morning, when we visit the garden, coffee cup in hand, to pick a ripe strawberry for breakfast. We dine on a shaded patio for lunch with a cool glass of rosé, and by the grill for dinner, when the early-evening amber light casts its glow. Spectacular pink and purple sunsets entertain us at table. For the second act, the stars come out one by one. Family-style platters are passed around the table, and wineglasses are filled and emptied and filled again. When the sun goes down and the evening cools, we don jackets and sweaters and sit around an outdoor fire.

It's so easy to cook in the summertime! The pressure is off. Meals are simple and delicious: a quick marinade on a steak or pork tenderloin, a colorful salad with the bounty of summer vegetables, and a dessert made with the luscious apricots, plums, or peaches we longed for in the dark days of winter. It's no problem at all to add another place setting or two, and guests bring baskets of homegrown fruit and vegetables from their orchards and gardens. We forget about the kitchen stove and focus on outdoor cooking.

The Summer Garden

Bounty! I don't know anyone who doesn't get excited about the summer garden. By the first of May, conversation in town swirls around planting. Have you gotten your tomatoes in yet? Who has the most interesting heirloom varieties? This year we'll plant fewer squash, and more peppers, or the other way around. We vow that this time we really will tame the gophers. We spend the whole weekend planting the garden, tossing off sweatshirts in the May sunshine, and the first sunburn appears on our bare arms. And we wait, not for very long, for the first baby vegetables to appear.

Even the first zucchini, practically loathed by late fall, is celebrated in June by every gardener I know. The first cucumbers are a revelation, so juicy and fresh. The first cherry tomatoes are like candy for children and grown-ups alike, portending the fat heirloom varieties to come. The early strawberries never make it out of the basket into the kitchen, but instead are eaten out of hand with pleasure. Young beans off the vine are tender enough to serve raw in a salad. And we check the height of our corn plants regularly. Are they knee-high by the Fourth of July? We rush home from work just to grab a basket and walk out into the garden, excited to harvest summer's dinner.

How do I pair wine with food?

First of all, I think this can be a confusing and paralyzing topic. I don't blame you if you want to just give up and open a few beers instead! Pairing wine and food should be fun and creative, and you should trust your own palate. The most challenging foods to pair with wine are those with high amounts of acid in them, whether lemon or lime juice or vinegar. Your best bet is to pick a wine with a zingy acidity, such as a Sauvignon Blanc or Pinot Gris. The second challenge is sweetness in food. Very sweet foods inevitably make a wine taste sour, unless of course, you're serving sweet wine. So again, your best bet with slightly sweet foods is to pick an aromatic and fruity white wine like a Riesling or a Gewürztraminer. A red Zinfandel has enough juicy fruit to work with slightly sweet foods as well.

Otherwise, the old rule of white wine with fish and chicken and red with beef can use a little updating. Grilled fish, with its smoky flavor, stands up quite nicely to a medium-bodied red like Pinot Noir. Chicken, whether roasted or grilled, does just fine with a fruity Merlot. Pork can be served with either red or white wine, so it's a foolproof option for entertaining. You can easily serve a Chardonnay as well as a more full-bodied red like Cabernet with pork, and everyone at your table will be happy. In the heat of summer, a chilled rosé makes a refreshing match with chicken, pork, and lamb.

Just remember to think in terms of going from light to rich. With delicate flavors, choose a more delicate wine. As your flavors become richer, so can your wines. A lush, creamy corn chowder, for example, would be great with a more full-flavored Chardonnay rather than a crisp Sauvignon Blanc. With bold flavors, go for a bold, full-flavored wine like a Cabernet Sauvignon or Syrah. The key is not to be intimidated, and to serve what you like.

Grillside Lunch

∘ ∘ ∘

Japanese Eggplant Salad with Sun Gold Tomatoes, Feta, and Mint / 76

Lamb Burgers on Potato Rolls with Aioli / 78

Grill-Roasted Summer Squash with Salsa Verde / 79

White Peach Crostata with Honey-Almond Ice Cream / 81

We put in an outdoor kitchen a couple of years ago, and now we live there during the summer. We've learned to grill just about everything. As an alternative to the ho-hum hamburger, we love the richer, more complex flavor of grilled lamb burgers. Go rustic red for wines with this menu—a Sonoma Tempranillo or Syrah would be just the ticket and can stand up to the smokiness of the grill. A Moscato or late-harvest Sauvignon Blanc makes a refreshing dessert accompaniment.

Japanese Eggplant Salad with Sun Gold Tomatoes, Feta, and Mint || SERVES 6

One year we planted six different varieties of eggplant, which even for me was probably too much! I like to use slender Japanese eggplants for this salad, as they hold their shape even on a grill. The key is not to overcook eggplant, or it will fall apart when you toss the salad. I've had good results roasting eggplant on a baking sheet as well.

Eggplant is a staple in the Mediterranean diet, and very wine friendly because of its creamy texture and flavor. It stands up to rustic red wines perfectly, so peppery Syrah is a nice match.

4 or 5 small Japanese eggplants/
aubergines, cut into 1-in/2.5-cm
diagonal slices

1 tbsp extra-virgin olive oil

½ tsp salt

¼ tsp freshly ground pepper

VINAIGRETTE

3 tbsp extra-virgin olive oil

1 tsp balsamic vinegar

1 tbsp fresh Meyer lemon juice

½ tsp salt

¼ tsp freshly ground pepper

2 cups/340 g Sun Gold tomatoes,
halved

1 cup/140 g crumbled feta cheese

2 cups/55 g arugula/rocket

1 tbsp finely chopped fresh mint

Preheat a gas grill/barbecue to medium-high, or prepare a medium-hot fire in a charcoal grill/barbecue.

In a medium bowl, toss the eggplant/aubergine in the olive oil, salt, and pepper. Grill over medium heat for 5 minutes on each side, or until just soft but not collapsed. If eggplant/aubergine is still not cooked through, reduce the heat, cover, and cook for 5 minutes more. Transfer to a plate and let cool completely.

For the vinaigrette: In a small bowl, whisk together the olive oil, vinegar, lemon juice, salt, and pepper.

In a large bowl, toss the cooled eggplant/aubergine with the tomatoes, feta, arugula/rocket, mint, and vinaigrette.

Lamb Burgers on Potato Rolls with Aioli   SERVES 6

My Syrian grandmother would make the butcher grind a leg of lamb for her to make kofta or kibbe, but ground lamb is readily available at the market these days, and perfect for these lamb burgers. Downtown Bakery in Healdsburg sells a gorgeous soft potato roll that just melts in your mouth but still supports a juicy burger. I also like to serve these burgers in pitas.

Lamb burgers are a wine country favorite because the savory lamb works so well with wine. The aioli packs a nice punch. Serve a bold Syrah to match the bold flavors of the dish.

1½ lb/680 g ground/minced lamb

2 shallots, finely chopped

2 garlic cloves, finely chopped

1 tbsp finely chopped fresh flat-leaf parsley

1 tbsp salt

1 tsp freshly ground pepper

AIOLI

3 garlic cloves, finely chopped

2 large egg yolks

Juice of 1 lemon

½ tsp salt

¼ tsp freshly ground pepper

1 cup/240 ml extra-virgin olive oil

6 potato rolls, halved horizontally, for serving

In a medium bowl, combine the lamb, shallots, garlic, parsley, salt, and pepper and mix until just combined. Shape into 6 patties. Set aside

For the aioli: Combine the garlic, egg yolks, lemon juice, salt, and pepper in a food processor. Pulse to combine. With the machine running, add the olive oil in a slow stream until emulsified. Taste and adjust the seasoning.

Preheat a gas grill/barbecue to medium-high, or prepare a medium-hot fire in a charcoal grill/barbecue.

Grill the burgers for 5 to 7 minutes per side for medium-rare. Toast the potato rolls, cut side down, for 1 minute. To serve, slather aioli on the toasted rolls and sandwich the burgers in between.

Grill-Roasted Summer Squash with Salsa Verde || SERVES 6

Once again, my garden overflows with summer squash. The trick is to pick them when young and slender, or about five inches long. I love them roasted with onions and thyme. I grew cipollini this year, small, disk-shaped Italian onions. They are wonderfully sweet and hold their shape when roasted. Shallots are a fine substitute.

It's much easier to grill vegetables on a rimmed baking sheet than directly on the grill. Who wants to be a slave to the grill while your guests are having fun?

12 small cipollini, peeled

2 tbsp extra-virgin olive oil

6 summer squash, sliced lengthwise into 1-in/2.5-cm pieces

Leaves from 4 to 6 thyme sprigs

1 tsp salt

½ tsp freshly ground pepper

SALSA VERDE

1 garlic clove, finely chopped

1 jalapeño chile, finely chopped

1 shallot, finely chopped

1 cup/40 g finely chopped mixed fresh flat-leaf parsley, cilantro/ fresh coriander, mint and/or basil

2 tbsp fresh lime juice

2 small anchovies, mashed

1 tsp salt

½ tsp freshly ground pepper

1 cup/240 ml extra-virgin olive oil

Preheat a gas grill/barbecue to high, or prepare a hot fire in a charcoal grill/barbecue.

On a rimmed baking sheet/tray, toss the onions with 1 tbsp of the oil. Place the pan on the grill/barbecue, cover, and roast the onions for 20 minutes, or until golden. Add the squash, the remaining 1 tbsp oil, the thyme, salt, and pepper and toss to coat. Roast for an additional 10 minutes, or until the squash is tender. Transfer the vegetables to a plate.

For the salsa verde: In a blender or food processor, combine the garlic, jalapeño, shallot, herbs, lime juice, anchovies, salt, and pepper. Blend until a paste is formed. With the machine running, drizzle in the olive oil in a slow stream until emulsified.

To serve, drizzle the salsa verde over the roasted vegetables.

White Peach Crostata with Honey-Almond Ice Cream ‖ SERVES 6

We have a white peach tree in our garden, and it's the first of the summer stone fruits to ripen, even before the apricots. We grab baskets and fill them full of these fragrant, delicate peaches. We eat as many as we can out of hand, sticky juice dribbling down our arms and chins. Homegrown white peaches don't last long in a fruit bowl and they bruise easily, so they are perfect for baking. The rest we peel, slice, and freeze for later use. It's amazing what a peach crisp or cobbler does for the spirits in midwinter!

This free-form tart lends itself to whatever stone fruit is in season and in abundance, whether peaches, nectarines, or plums. Leave the peels on the nectarines and plums, but do peel the peaches. The tart dough can be made a day or two ahead of time and kept in the refrigerator. Just roll it out and fill when you're ready to bake.

In the summertime, a little ice-cold dessert wine is a sweet and refreshing way to end a meal. Choose a late-harvest Sauvignon Blanc here, or if you like bubbles, a slightly effervescent Moscato.

TART DOUGH

1¼ cups/250 g all-purpose/plain flour

⅛ tsp salt

2 tsp sugar

7 tbsp/100 g cold unsalted butter, cut into chunks

3 tbsp ice water

FILLING

2 tbsp sugar

1 tsp cornstarch/cornflour

4 to 5 white peaches, peeled, pitted, and cut into 1-in/2.5-cm slices

1 tbsp fresh lemon juice

½ tsp vanilla extract/essence

1 large egg, beaten

Honey-Almond Ice Cream (page 83) for serving

continued

For the dough: Pulse the flour, salt, and sugar in a food processor until blended. Add the chunks of butter and blend just until mixture resembles pebbles. Add the ice water 1 tbsp at a time and pulse just until the mixture comes together. Do not let form into a ball. Turn out onto a floured surface and shape into a disk. Wrap in plastic wrap and refrigerate for 30 minutes or up 2 days.

For the filling: In a large bowl, stir together the sugar and cornstarch/cornflour to combine. Stir in the peaches, lemon juice, and vanilla. Let stand for about 30 minutes to release the juices.

Adjust an oven rack in the center of the oven. Preheat the oven to 375°F/190°C/gas 5. Remove the dough from the refrigerator and let soften for a few minutes. Roll the dough out onto a piece of parchment/baking paper to 12 in/20.5 cm in diameter, then place the parchment/baking paper, with the dough, on a baking sheet/tray. Pile the fruit mixture into the center and fold the edges of the dough up around the fruit, pinching to make a seam every 2 in/5 cm. There should be at least 6 in/15 cm of fruit showing. Brush the edges of the dough liberally with the beaten egg.

Bake for 45 to 50 minutes, or until the crust is golden brown and the fruit is bubbling at the edges. Transfer to a wire rack and let cool slightly or completely. Remove the sides of the pan, cut the tart into wedges, and serve with the honey-almond ice cream.

ASK THE WINEMAKER

How do I store my wine?

The good news is that you don't need a fancy cellar at perfect temperature in order to safely store your wine, although if you're lucky enough to have one, enjoy it! Ideally, wine should be cellared at 55° to 60°F/13° to 16°C. However, if you have a basement that doesn't fluctuate wildly in temperature, that's fine, too, even if it's slightly warmer than 60°F/13°C. The countertop wine refrigerators found at home stores are inexpensive. Even the under-counter ones have come down in price, and are a nice alternative to a cellar. The biggest enemy to wine is heat, so don't store your wine above your refrigerator, which tends to be the warmest part of the kitchen. Even a dark closet will do.

Once a bottle is opened, store it in the refrigerator, whether white or red. Refrigeration will reduce oxidation. If it's a red wine, just remove it from the fridge half an hour before serving so it can get to cellar temperature again. You can invest in one of those devices that pump the oxygen out of a bottle, which will prolong the life of an opened bottle of wine. But in my house, a bottle rarely lasts more than two days. Past that, I use it as cooking wine.

Honey-Almond Ice Cream || MAKES 1½ QT/1.4 L

We keep bees on our property. My husband Jake is the chief beekeeper. With his bee suit, mask, and gloves, he is a sight to behold as he removes the honeycomb frames to extract the precious amber-hued liquid. The bees feast on our lavender, fruit tree blossoms, and any other pollen they can find up to a three-mile radius. We show gratitude for our neighbors' flower gardens by dropping off jars of honey.

Thanks to the bees, I substitute more and more honey for sugar in my desserts. This ice cream is a perfect example, and almonds and honey is an ancient match.

So dust off that ice cream maker lurking in the back of your cabinet! Ice cream is really fun to make with kids, and the flavor combinations are endless.

2½ cups/600 ml heavy/double cream
2 cups/480 ml whole milk

¼ cup/85 g almond paste, cut into small chunks
1 tsp almond extract/essence

8 large egg yolks
¾ cup/60 ml honey
¼ tsp salt

In a medium saucepan, combine the cream, milk, and almond paste. Cook over medium-high heat for 5 minutes, or until bubbles form around the edges of the pan. Do not let simmer. Remove from heat, add the almond extract, cover, and let stand for 30 minutes.

Using an electric mixer, beat the egg yolks, honey, and salt at high speed until the mixture has doubled in volume. Reduce the speed to medium. Gradually beat in 1 cup/ 240 ml of the cream mixture to temper. Again add 1 cup/

240 ml of the mixture and beat to combine. Return to the saucepan and cook over low heat, stirring often, until the mixture is thick enough to coat the back of a spoon, about 5 minutes. Strain the custard into a medium bowl set into an ice bath, and let cool. Cover and refrigerate for at least 2 hours or overnight.

Freeze in an ice cream maker according to the manufacturer's instructions.

Summer Dinner Under the Stars

○ ○ ○

Cucumber Salad with Mâche and Ricotta Salata / 85

Ginger and Lime–Grilled Halibut with Nectarine Salsa / 86

Spicy Summer Corn Pudding / 88

Fragrant Zucchini with Mustard Seeds / 89

Wild Blackberry–Thyme Crisp with Pistachio Ice Cream / 90

We have several friends who are avid fishermen, so this menu is a summer standby for the catch of the day. My version of camping is to grill and eat dinner outside, then retire to my own comfortable bed! I love to grill halibut. Its thick white fillets keep their shape, and the grill marks look beautiful against the white flesh. Just make sure to oil your grill so the fillets don't stick.

As for wine, a floral Viognier works with the sweet heat of the nectarine salsa, and matches the richness of the halibut. If you're wanting red, a juicy Pinot Noir is always a good match for grilled fish because of its lighter tannins. You might opt to go easy on the nectarine salsa, though, as its sweetness will make red wine taste a bit tart.

Cucumber Salad with Mâche and Ricotta Salata | SERVES 6

Cucumbers are the first of the summer vegetables to appear in my garden, and they are a cause for celebration indeed. We eat the small ones whole, peel and all, as snacks. This salad lets the cucumbers be the star, supported by mâche, otherwise known as lamb's lettuce, as the leaves are said to resemble lambs' tongues. Ricotta salata is a sheep's milk ricotta that has been aged until firm and crumbly. It has a wonderful nutty taste that is a nice foil to the fresh flavors of cucumber and mâche. I like to use Armenian cucumbers because their seeds are quite small and the flesh very firm. They have pale green peels and flesh. If you grow them, pick them when still young and slender. They will grow to be gargantuan if you let them! You may substitute an English cucumber instead.

The Viognier will work nicely with the salad because of the salty richness of the ricotta salata.

2 small Armenian cucumbers, peeled and thinly sliced

1 bunch mâche (about 2 cups/55 g)

2 oz/55 g ricotta salata, crumbled

¼ cup/60 ml extra-virgin olive oil

2 tsp Champagne vinegar

½ tsp salt

¼ tsp freshly ground pepper

In a medium salad bowl, combine the cucumbers, mâche, and ricotta salata. In a small bowl, whisk together the oil, vinegar, salt, and pepper. Toss the salad with the vinaigrette and divide among salad plates.

Ginger and Lime-Grilled Halibut with Nectarine Salsa | SERVES 6

Mango salsa was one of my very first grown-up recipes, conjured sometime in the late, great eighties. I've brought it into the new millennium by using summer nectarines. Their sweetness and acidity are a welcome foil for the spicy jalapeños and fresh herbs. Besides, our tree really puts out in the summer, and there are only so many nectarine crisps and tarts a family can eat! This salsa complements chicken and pork tenderloin, too.

Although the halibut works beautifully with an aromatic Viognier, the smoky flavor of the grilled fish makes it a great match for a juicy red wine like Pinot Noir.

Grated zest and juice of 1 lime

1 tbsp grated peeled fresh ginger

¼ cup/60 ml extra-virgin olive oil

1 tsp salt

½ tsp freshly ground pepper

Six 4-oz/115-g halibut fillets, skinned

NECTARINE SALSA

2 nectarines, pitted and cut into ½-in/12-mm dice

1 red bell pepper/capsicum, seeded, deveined, and cut into ½-in/12-mm dice

¼ cup/10 g chopped fresh cilantro/ fresh coriander

1 jalapeño chile, seeded and finely chopped

2 tbsp fresh lime juice

1 tbsp extra-virgin olive oil

½ tsp salt

¼ tsp freshly ground pepper

In a medium bowl, combine the lime zest and juice, ginger, olive oil, salt, and pepper. Stir to blend. Pour into a large, heavy self-sealing plastic bag and add the fish. Close the bag and refrigerate for at least 1 hour or up to 3 hours, turning several times.

Meanwhile, for the salsa: In a medium bowl, combine all the ingredients and let stand at room temperature.

Preheat a gas grill/barbecue to medium-high, or prepare a medium-hot fire in a charcoal grill/barbecue. Oil the grill well and grill the halibut for 5 to 7 minutes on each side, or until opaque throughout.

Serve the fillets topped with the salsa.

Spicy Summer Corn Pudding ‖ SERVES 6

For some strange reason, my family does not like corn on the cob. Go figure. However, they adore fresh corn in this pudding, and we fight for the last spoonfuls. The sweetness of summer corn gets a bright lift from cilantro, sweet peppers, and chiles. The classic Mexican cheese queso fresco is widely available here in Sonoma, but Monterey Jack may be substituted. This is the only dish on the menu that requires an oven. Make it in the early morning before the house gets hot, then reheat it on a warm, not hot, grill. Believe me; it's worth it.

The sweetness of the corn works perfectly with the sweet, aromatic flavors of Viognier.

4 tbsp/55 g unsalted butter

1 yellow onion, chopped

1 red bell pepper/capsicum, seeded, deveined, and finely chopped

3 scallions, finely chopped

1 jalapeño chile, finely chopped

4 cups/680 g white corn kernels (about 6 ears corn)

3 large eggs

1½ cups/360 ml half-and-half/ half cream

2 tbsp chopped fresh cilantro/ fresh coriander

1 tbsp salt

½ tsp freshly ground black pepper

½ tsp chili powder

1 cup/140 g crumbled queso fresco

Preheat the oven to 375°F/190°C/gas 5. Butter an 8-cup/2-l gratin dish.

In a large sauté pan, melt the butter over medium heat just until foaming. Add the onion and sauté until translucent, about 3 minutes. Add the bell pepper/capsicum, scallions, and jalapeño and sauté for 2 minutes. Add the corn and sauté for 2 minutes more. Remove from heat and set aside.

In a large bowl, whisk together the eggs and half-and-half/ half cream. Stir in the cilantro/fresh coriander, salt, pepper, chili powder, and ½ cup/70 g of the cheese, then the cooked corn mixture. Pour into the prepared dish. Sprinkle the top with the remaining ½ cup/70 g cheese.

Place the gratin dish in a large roasting pan/tray and fill the pan with boiling water to reach halfway up the sides of the dish. Bake the pudding for 40 minutes, or until a knife inserted in the center comes out clean. Serve warm.

Fragrant Zucchini with Mustard Seeds ||

Once August hits, we're desperate for new ways to use zucchini. Even the tried-and-true barter system doesn't work around here, as every gardener I know has too much zucchini on hand. Here's an exotic twist on sautéed zucchini, with fragrant mustard seeds contributing the top note. This dish can be made ahead and served at room temperature, although it's delicious warm as well.

White wines are great with Indian food, so it's no surprise that Viognier works nicely with this dish. But the earthiness of mustard seeds matches the Pinot Noir as well.

1 tbsp extra-virgin olive oil

1 tbsp mustard seeds

1 large garlic clove, finely chopped

6 small zucchini/courgettes, cut into 1-in/2.5-cm diagonal pieces

1 tsp salt

½ tsp freshly ground pepper

In a large sauté pan or frying pan, heat the olive oil over medium heat until just shimmering. Add the mustard seeds and cook until they pop, about 2 minutes. Add the garlic and sauté for 1 minute. Add the zucchini/courgettes, salt, and pepper and toss to coat. Reduce heat to medium-low, cover, and cook for 5 minutes, or until crisp-tender.

Wild Blackberry-Thyme Crisp with Pistachio Ice Cream || SERVES 6

Blackberries grow wild on our country road. We head out, baskets in hand, and after an hour or two of pricked fingers and stained hands, return home with just enough for a crisp. I've added fragrant thyme to the blackberries for a more sophisticated flavor. I love the combination of winey blackberries and pistachio ice cream, but good old vanilla is a classic option.

4 cups/455 g fresh blackberries

1 tbsp cornstarch/cornflour

⅓ cup/65 g sugar

1 tsp finely chopped fresh thyme

1 tbsp fresh lemon juice

1 tsp vanilla extract/essence

TOPPING

6 tbsp/45 g all-purpose/plain flour

½ cup/100 g packed brown sugar/ Demerara sugar

½ cup/100 g granulated sugar

¼ tsp ground cinnamon

¼ tsp freshly grated nutmeg

½ tsp salt

6 tbsp/85 g cold unsalted butter, cut into chunks

Pistachio ice cream (facing page) for serving

Adjust an oven rack in the center of the oven. Preheat the oven to 375°F/190°C/gas 5. In a large bowl, gently toss the blackberries with the cornstarch/cornflour, sugar, thyme, lemon juice, and vanilla. Let stand for 15 minutes while you make the topping.

For the topping: In a food processor, pulse the flour, sugars, cinnamon, nutmeg, and salt until combined. Add the butter and process until the mixture resembles coarse sand.

Turn the fruit out into a 9-in/23-cm baking dish. Top evenly with the topping. Bake for 45 minutes, or until the fruit is bubbling and the topping is golden brown.

Serve warm, with the ice cream.

Pistachio Ice Cream | MAKES 1½ QT/1.4 L

1 cup unsalted shelled pistachios

2½ cups/600 ml heavy/double cream

2 cups/480 ml whole milk

½ teaspoon almond extract/essence

8 large egg yolks

¾ cup sugar

¼ tsp salt

Grind the pistachios finely in a food processor or spice grinder.

In a medium saucepan, combine the cream, milk, and ground pistachios. Cook over low heat for 5 minutes, or until bubbles form around the edges of the pan. Do not let simmer. Remove from heat and add the almond extract/essence. Cover and let stand for 30 minutes.

Using an electric mixer, beat the egg yolks, sugar, and salt at high speed until the mixture has doubled in volume. Reduce the speed to medium. Gradually beat in 1 cup/240 ml of the cream mixture to temper. Again add 1 cup/240 ml of the mixture and beat to combine. Return to the saucepan and cook over low heat, stirring often, until the mixture is thick enough to coat the back of a spoon, about 5 minutes. Remove from heat, and strain into a medium bowl set in an ice bath. Let cool completely. Cover and refrigerate for at least 2 hours or overnight.

Freeze in an ice cream maker according to the manufacturer's instructions.

ASK THE WINEMAKER

*When someone brings a bottle of wine to my dinner party,
should I serve it that night?*

There's no need to serve wine that's been brought as a gift, unless you're short on wine and need another bottle to go around. When invited to someone's house, I always ask what I can bring, and invariably the host asks me to bring wine. In that case, I assume that we'll be drinking that wine for dinner, and I ask about the menu to make sure the wine I bring will work. If there are more than six people at the dinner party, and you're asked to bring wine, bring two bottles so there's enough to go around. Even if you need to choose a less expensive wine, it's better to have enough for everyone than to bring an expensive wine that doesn't quite make it through a course.

Pizza Party

○ ○ ○

Smoked Duck, Picholine, and Pecorino Pizza / 95

Wild Nettle and Taleggio Pizza / 97

Summer Tomato, Basil, and Fresh Ricotta Pizza / 98

Arugula and Pine Nut Salad / 100

Scharffen Berger Brownies with Espresso Ice Cream / 101

After years of making pizza in the oven, waiting for the temperature to rise before the smoke alarm in the kitchen went off, we tried doing pizzas outside on the grill. We've never looked back. Turn all the grill burners up to high or make a hot charcoal fire, close the lid, and let the grill get as hot as it can. You'll get a crisp crust with slightly smoky grill marks, and the toppings will cook beautifully.

This is a great party for a crowd, as everyone can top their own pizzas to their liking. These are small pizzas, so count on each one serving two or three people.

There's nothing more welcoming at a summer outdoor party than a big ice bucket full of chilled bottles of dry rosé from Napa or Sonoma. A bold Dry Creek Zinfandel will complement the grill flavors of the pizza.

Smoked Duck, Picholine, and Pecorino Pizza ‖ SERVES 2 TO 3

This pizza fits squarely into the gourmet department. Once you've got the dough made, it's all about assembly. You can find delicious smoked duck at a specialty foods market or deli. Pit the olives, shave some pecorino cheese, and you're good to go. You may add some extra toppings, depending on how liberally you like to top your pizza.

Serve this duck pizza with a dry rosé. The fruitiness of the wine is a great foil to the saltiness of the olives and the smokiness of the duck.

2 tbsp extra-virgin olive oil

1 small garlic clove, finely chopped

1 tsp salt

½ tsp freshly ground pepper

One 12-in/30-cm Pizza Dough round (page 96)

½ cup/60 g grated pecorino cheese

4 oz/115 g smoked duck, thinly sliced

¼ cup/30 g pitted picholine olives, quartered

Preheat a gas grill/barbecue to the highest temperature possible, or prepare a hot fire in a charcoal grill/barbecue.

In a small bowl, combine the olive oil, garlic, salt, and pepper. Brush the garlic oil liberally over the entire dough round. Scatter the cheese evenly over the dough. Add the duck and olives.

Place the dough directly on the grill/barbecue grids, cover, and cook until the crust is browned and the cheese is bubbling, 5 to 8 minutes.

Pizza Dough

½ cup/120 ml plus ¾ cup/180 ml warm (105° to 115°F/40° to 46°C) water

1 package (2¼ tsp) active dry yeast

2 tbsp extra-virgin olive oil

4 cups/450 g all-purpose/plain flour

1 tbsp salt

Measure the ½ cup/120 ml warm water into a 2-cup/480-ml glass measure. Sprinkle the yeast over, stir to dissolve, and let stand until foamy, about 5 minutes. Add the ¾ cup/180 ml warm water and the oil.

Combine the flour and salt in a food processor. With the machine running, add the yeast mixture and process for several minutes until the dough forms a sticky ball.

Turn out the dough onto a floured surface and knead several times until the dough is smooth and elastic. Place in a large, well-oiled bowl and turn to coat the dough completely with oil. Cover with plastic wrap and let rise in a warm place for 2 hours, or until doubled. If not using the dough immediately, wrap the dough in plastic wrap and place in the refrigerator for up to 2 days.

Turn the dough out onto a lightly floured surface and divide into 4 pieces. Roll and press each into a 12-in/30-cm round.

ASK THE WINEMAKER

What's all the fuss about pink wine? I see more and more of it in my market and wine shop, but I thought it was sweet.

Rosé wine is a great pleasure, one that those lucky to live in the south of France indulge in on a regular basis amid their lavender fields and boules courts. In the United States, our association with pink wine started with the unfortunate white Zinfandel, which is loaded with sugar and not very interesting. The saving grace is that it introduced wine to a whole generation of college students, who have graduated from white Zin picnics to candlelit dinners accompanied with cult Cabernet.

Proper rosé, made famous by those Provençal winemakers, is generally made from red grapes, like Grenache or Syrah, and is dry rather than sweet. Its fruity, thirst-quenching flavor makes it perfect for a hot summer day and equally at home with seafood or a grilled leg of lamb. Its California counterpart may also be made of Pinot Noir or Merlot. The grapes are picked earlier than for red wine, and sit with their skins on for a day or so to yield a lovely pink juice. More acidic than red wine, rosé is the ultimate thirst quencher, and a great alternative to those who tire of white wine in the summer months. Rosé matches beautifully with rosy lamb, pork, and chicken. It works nicely with spicy foods, too. Best of all, it tends to not be expensive, so you can pop corks or twist screw caps with abandon. Rosé is a nice option at Thanksgiving as well, as its fruitiness works nicely with the slightly sweet palate of the menu.

Wild Nettle and Taleggio Pizza ||

This cheesy pizza boasts the sophisticated taste of Taleggio, a creamy Italian cow's milk cheese. Make sure the Taleggio is very cold when you cut it; otherwise, it will stick to your knife. Wild nettles grow all over our property, and it's comforting to know that though they wreak havoc in my flower beds, they're also good eating. Be sure to wear rubber gloves to harvest and clean them, or they will sting your hands.

The richness of Taleggio calls for an equally lusty Zinfandel.

2 tbsp extra-virgin olive oil

1 small garlic clove, finely chopped

1 tsp salt

½ tsp freshly ground pepper

One 12-in/30-cm Pizza Dough round (facing page)

4 oz/115 g Taleggio cheese, cut into thin slices

2 cups/60 g coarsely chopped wild nettles

Preheat a gas grill/barbecue to the highest temperature possible, or prepare a hot fire in a charcoal grill/barbecue.

In a small bowl, combine the oil, garlic, salt, and pepper. Place the dough round on a pizza peel dusted with cornmeal. Brush the garlic oil liberally over the dough round.

Scatter the Taleggio cheese evenly over the dough and then scatter the nettles over.

Slide the dough directly onto the grill/barbecue grids. Cover and cook until the crust is browned and the cheese is bubbling, 5 to 8 minutes.

Summer Tomato, Basil, and Fresh Ricotta Pizza || SERVES 2 TO 3

Where are the tomatoes, you say? Never fear, they're here, thinly sliced. No gloppy tomato pasty sauce on my pizzas! Roma tomatoes work best, as their meatiness stands up to high heat on the grill. This recipe uses the earliest of the summer tomatoes, fragrant basil, and creamy ricotta for a sublime pizza.

The acidity of the tomatoes is a good match with a dry rosé, but the richness of ricotta is complemented by a bold red like Zinfandel, too.

2 tbsp extra-virgin olive oil

1 small garlic clove, minced

1 tsp salt

½ tsp freshly ground pepper

One 12-in/30-cm Pizza Dough round (page 96)

4 oz/115 g fresh whole-milk ricotta cheese

2 tomatoes, thinly sliced

¼ cup/10 g very thinly sliced fresh basil

Preheat a gas grill/barbecue to the highest temperature you can, or prepare a hot fire in a charcoal grill/barbecue.

In a small bowl, combine the olive oil, garlic, salt, and pepper. Place the dough round on a pizza peel dusted lightly with cornmeal. Brush the garlic oil liberally over the entire dough round.

Spread the ricotta evenly all over the pizza. Place the tomatoes on the pizza, then scatter the basil evenly over the top.

Slide the dough directly on the grill/barbecue grids, cover, and cook until the crust is browned and the cheese is bubbling, 5 to 8 minutes.

Arugula and Pine Nut Salad || SERVES 6

Arugula grows year-round in our garden, and I love its peppery taste
in salads. This salad, a simple combination of arugula and toasted pine
nuts, is the perfect accompaniment to pizza. A red wine and balsamic
vinaigrette is the only adornment it needs.

½ cup/55 g pine nuts

¼ cup/60 g extra-virgin olive oil

1 tbsp red wine vinegar

1 tsp balsamic vinegar

½ tsp salt

¼ tsp freshly ground pepper

4 cups/115 g torn arugula/rocket

Preheat the oven to 350°F/180°C/gas 4. In a rimmed
baking sheet/tray, spread the pine nuts in a single layer.
Toast for 10 minutes, or until golden brown. Remove
from the oven, pour into a bowl, and let cool.

In a small bowl, whisk together the oil, vinegars, salt, and
pepper. In a large salad bowl, toss the arugula/rocket and
pine nuts with the dressing and serve.

Scharffen Berger Brownies with Espresso Ice Cream | MAKES 24 BROWNIES

John Scharffenberger and Robert Steinberg began making exquisite artisanal chocolate in South San Francisco in 1997; today, Scharffen Berger chocolate is distributed all over the country and is owned by Hershey. Scharffen Berger's dark chocolate bars and cocoa set an international standard, previously held only by European brands. John was a vintner prior to becoming a chocolatier. Though he has since sold the Mendocino winery, Scharffenberger sparkling wine continues to be a favorite.

This recipe uses Scharffen Berger cocoa powder and chopped chocolate bars for brownies that never fail to please. In lieu of coffee at the end of this summer meal, pair the brownies with homemade espresso ice cream. The designated drivers will thank you.

1 cup/130 g all-purpose/plain flour

½ tsp baking powder

½ tsp salt

1 cup/225 g unsalted butter, melted

2 cups/400 g sugar

2 tsp vanilla extract/essence

4 large eggs

¾ cup/60 g Scharffen Berger unsweetened cocoa powder

1 cup walnuts, chopped

10 oz/280 g Scharffen Berger bittersweet chocolate, chopped

Espresso Ice Cream (page 102) for serving

Adjust an oven rack in the center of the oven. Preheat the oven to 350°F/180°C/gas 4. Butter a 9-by-13-in/ 23-by-33-cm baking pan.

Sift the flour, baking powder, and salt together into a medium bowl.

In the bowl of a stand mixer fitted with the paddle attachment, combine the butter and sugar and beat to combine. Beat in the vanilla, then the eggs, one at a time, scraping down the sides of the bowl after each addition. Add the cocoa and beat gently. In two additions, beat in the flour mixture just until incorporated. Add the nuts and chocolate and stir to combine.

Scrape the batter into the prepared pan and smooth the top. Bake for 40 to 45 minutes, or until the sides have pulled away from the pan and the top is cracked; a toothpick inserted in the center will have moist crumbs attached. Remove from the oven and let cool in the pan on a wire rack/cake cooler. Cut into 24 squares to serve.

Serve with Espresso Ice Cream.

Espresso Ice Cream || MAKES 1½ QT/1.4 L

2½ cups/600 ml heavy/double cream
2 cups/480 ml whole milk

4 tsp instant espresso powder
8 large egg yolks

¾ cup/150 g sugar
¼ tsp salt

In a medium saucepan, combine the cream, milk, and espresso powder. Cook over low heat for 5 minutes, or until bubbles form around the edges of the pan. Do not simmer. Remove from heat, cover, and let stand for 30 minutes.

Using an electric mixer, beat the egg yolks, sugar, and salt at high speed until the mixture has doubled in volume. Reduce the speed to medium. Gradually beat in 1 cup/ 240 ml of the cream mixture to temper. Again add 1 cup/240 ml of the mixture and beat to combine. Return to the saucepan and cook over low heat, stirring often, until the mixture is thick enough to coat the back of a spoon, about 5 minutes. Remove from heat and strain into a medium bowl set in an ice bath. Let cool completely. Cover and refrigerate for at least 2 hours or overnight.

Freeze in an ice cream maker according to the manufacturer's instructions.

Eastern Mediterranean Feast

∘ ∘ ∘

Summer, with all its tomatoes, eggplants/aubergines, and peppers/capsicums, calls out for a Mediterranean feast. This meal revolves around a delicious Lebanese street food called shawarma. Grilled marinated lamb is sliced thin and served in homemade pita with a lovely yogurt sauce. You could start with a zingy Sauvignon Blanc, and pour lots of peppery Sonoma Syrah to pair with the lamb.

Muhammara with Armenian Cucumbers || SERVES 8 TO 12

Muhammara is a red pepper/capsicum and walnut dip that hails from Aleppo, in northern Syria, famous for its hot and sweet Aleppo peppers. The dip is a gorgeous brick red and is at once creamy, salty, and spicy. I adore it with the crunch of Armenian cucumber spears. My dear friend Honore requires her very own bowl when she comes to dinner. It's addictive!

If you can't find ground Aleppo pepper, you can substitute cayenne. Pomegranate molasses, tart and only slightly sweet, is available at specialty foods markets. You can also order the Sultan brand online at www.ethnicgrocer.com, or reduce pomegranate juice until syrupy.

A lively Sauvignon Blanc is the perfect answer to the brightness of the peppers and tart sweetness of the pomegranate molasses in this dish.

2 large red bell peppers/capsicums

1½ cups/170 g walnut halves

½ cup/40 g crushed stoned wheat crackers

1 tbsp fresh lemon juice

2 tbsp pomegranate molasses

½ tsp ground cumin

½ tsp ground Aleppo pepper

1 tsp salt

½ tsp freshly ground black pepper

2 tbsp extra-virgin olive oil, plus more for drizzling

1 tbsp chopped fresh flat-leaf parsley

4 Armenian cucumbers, peeled and cut into spears 3 in/7.5 cm long

Preheat a gas grill/barbecue to medium-high, or prepare a medium-hot fire in a charcoal grill/barbecue. Roast the bell peppers/capsicums on the grill, turning frequently, until blistered all over. Place in a covered bowl or paper bag and let cool for 15 minutes. Remove the skin, seeds, and veins.

In a food processor, grind the walnuts, crackers, lemon juice, and pomegranate molasses until the mixture forms a thick, smooth paste. Add the cumin, Aleppo pepper, salt, and black pepper and process until smooth. Add the roasted vegetables and puree until creamy. With the machine running, gradually add the 2 tbsp olive oil until emulsified. Taste and adjust the seasoning.

Serve in a small dish, drizzled with olive oil and garnished with parsley, with the cucumber spears on the side.

Sonoma Shawarma with Tahini-Yogurt Sauce and Syrian Pita || SERVES 8 TO 12

This dish is my version of the Middle Eastern street food classic. Rather than roast the lamb on a spit, I grill a marinated boneless leg of lamb and serve slices on pita with caramelized onions, sweet peppers, and a creamy tahini sauce. The quality of the pita makes all the difference. It really isn't hard to make your own, and the flavor and texture are far superior to the flaccid, sweet-tasting brand you find in most grocery stores. If you don't want to make your own, do seek out pita from a specialty, Middle Eastern, or Indian grocer.

This is also a great dish for a crowd. We made shawarma for thirty people for our son's third birthday, and it was a hit with both parents and kids. Forget forks and knives. Hands are the best tools; just fold the shawarma like a taco and enjoy. But keep plenty of napkins nearby!

Ask your butcher to butterfly a leg of lamb for you, making it as flat as possible in order to grill evenly. Once you get it home, you can pound it to a more uniform thickness. But don't worry if it's not completely flat. The thicker parts will be medium-rare once cooked, and the thinner sections medium for those guests who don't like their meat pink.

A Sonoma, Napa, or Paso Robles Syrah, made from a grape indigenous to Persia, is the wine of choice for this dish.

MARINADE

1 cup/240 ml extra-virgin olive oil

Juice of 2 lemons

6 garlic cloves, minced

1 tbsp ground cumin

1 tbsp ground cardamom

1½ tbsp salt

1 tsp freshly ground black pepper

1 tsp ground Aleppo or cayenne pepper

One 7-lb/3.2-kg leg of lamb, boned and butterflied

SAUTÉED ONIONS

3 large red onions, halved lengthwise

¼ cup/60 ml extra-virgin olive oil

SAUTÉED PEPPERS

2 orange bell peppers/capsicums

1 yellow bell pepper/capsicum

1 tbsp extra-virgin olive oil

½ tsp salt

¼ tsp freshly ground black pepper

Syrian Pita (page 109) for serving

Tahini-Yogurt Sauce (recipe follows) for serving

continued

For the marinade: Combine all the ingredients in a large, heavy self-sealing plastic bag. Add the lamb, seal, and refrigerate overnight or preferably for 2 days, turning the bag occasionally.

Preheat a gas grill/barbecue to medium-high heat, or prepare a medium-hot fire in a charcoal grill/barbecue. Grill the lamb for 8 to 10 minutes per side for medium rare, with the grill covered. Transfer to a carving board, tent with aluminum foil, and let rest for 10 minutes.

While the lamb is cooking, prepare the onions and peppers. For the onions: Place the onions, cut side down, on a cutting board and cut into thin crosswise slices. In a large sauté pan or frying pan, heat the olive oil over medium heat until shimmering. Reduce heat to low, add the onions, and sauté until caramelized, stirring occasionally, about 20 minutes. Remove from heat and set aside.

For the peppers: Cut all the bell peppers/capsicums in half lengthwise; discard the seeds and veins. Cut the peppers lengthwise into ½-in/12-mm strips. In a medium sauté pan or frying pan, heat the olive oil over medium-high heat until shimmering. Add the bell peppers/capsicums, salt, and black pepper and sauté until crisp-tender, 5 to 7 minutes. Remove from heat and set aside.

To serve, while the lamb is resting, wrap a stack of pita in aluminum foil, place on the grill/barbecue, and cover to warm. Cut the lamb into thin slices. Place a warm pita on each plate. Top with several slices of lamb, then caramelized onions, then peppers. Drizzle the sauce over the top.

Tahini-Yogurt Sauce   ‖ MAKES ABOUT 2 CUPS/480 ML

¼ cup/70 g tahini (sesame paste)

Juice of ½ lemon

1 tbsp extra-virgin olive oil

2 cups/480 ml plain whole-milk yogurt

1 tsp ground cumin

1 tsp salt

½ tsp ground Aleppo or cayenne pepper

1 tbsp finely chopped fresh flat-leaf parsley

In a medium bowl, whisk together the tahini, lemon juice, and oil until smooth. Whisk in the yogurt, then the cumin, salt, and pepper. Use now, or cover and refrigerate for up to 2 days. Stir in the parsley just before serving.

Syrian Pita ‖ MAKES 12 PITAS

This recipe is adapted from my Grandmother Louise's recipe. My sisters and I learned to knead dough and wield a baker's peel at her elbow. We'd wake up early and spend hours in her kitchen making an enormous batch of bread. We'd eat the first pitas right out of the oven with melted butter. She'd set aside half a dozen loaves for eating that week, and freeze the rest for later use.

½ cup/120 ml warm (105° to 115°F/40° to 45°C) water

1 package (2¼ tsp) active dry yeast

1 cup/240 ml warm (105° to 115°F/40° to 45°C) milk

4 cups/500 g bread/strong flour

1 tsp salt

2 tbsp extra-virgin olive oil

Add the warm water to a 2-cup/480-ml glass measure. Sprinkle the yeast over and stir until dissolved. Let stand until foamy, about 5 minutes. Stir in the warm milk.

In a food processor, pulse the flour and salt until combined. Gradually pour in the yeast mixture and process until the dough forms a ball.

Turn the dough out on a floured surface and give it a few quick kneads to shape it into a ball. Brush the dough all over with the olive oil. Place in an oiled large bowl, cover with plastic wrap or a damp towel, and let rise in a warm place for 2 hours, or until doubled. Turn the dough out on a floured surface and divide in half. Divide each half into 6 pieces and form each into a ball. Place on a

floured baking sheet/tray, cover with plastic wrap, and let rise for 20 minutes.

Roll out each ball to a round 4 to 5 in/12 to 12 cm in diameter. Don't worry about making a perfect round. Using a sharp knife, make a few 1-in/2.5-cm slashes in each round.

Preheat a gas grill/barbecue to high, or prepare a hot fire in a charcoal grill/barbecue. Dust a pizza peel or baking sheet/tray with flour. Place the dough rounds, one at a time, on the pizza peel or pan and transfer to the grill/barbecue. Grill on each side for 2 to 3 minutes, or until the bread has grill marks and is cooked through.

Early Girl Tomato Salad with Feta and Mint ‖ SERVES 8 TO 10

Once we get our tomato plants in the ground, sometime in early May, we mark their progress each day, waiting for the flowers to turn to green fruit and then from blush to ruby red. There is nothing that removes the stress of a long workday better than a trip out to the garden to see what's ripe. We're giddy at the prospect of our first basket of homegrown tomatoes.

In this salad, the first summer tomatoes are paired with briny feta and fresh mint. I like to use Greek feta in this salad because of the Mediterranean flavors of the menu. French feta, milder and creamier, is not quite right here.

A simple olive oil and lemon dressing is spiked with a little balsamic to make it more wine friendly. The sweetness of the balsamic tempers the acidity of the lemon and makes this salad a lovely match for crisp Sauvignon Blanc.

¼ cup/60 ml extra-virgin olive oil

2 tbsp fresh lemon juice

1 tsp balsamic vinegar

½ tsp salt

¼ tsp freshly ground pepper

8 tomatoes, cut into wedges

1 cup/140 g crumbled Greek feta cheese

¼ cup/5 g finely chopped fresh mint

In a small bowl, whisk together the oil, lemon juice, vinegar, salt, and pepper. Arrange the tomato wedges on a platter. Scatter the feta on top, then the mint. Drizzle with the dressing and serve.

Honey-Roasted Apricots with Almonds || SERVES 8 TO 10

Apricots are a staple in the eastern Mediterranean, so I've used them as the final note to this menu. We have an apricot tree that yields a small number of little jewels. But even if you don't grow your own, apricots are an early-summer treat not to be missed. They arrive in the market in June and disappear with alarming swiftness, so grab them while you can. Roasting concentrates their sweetness and flavor, and the honey and almonds are a perfect accompaniment.

3 tbsp unsalted butter

¼ cup honey

3 tbsp white dessert wine, such as Muscat

16 small ripe apricots, halved and pitted

1 cup/115 g coarsely chopped almonds

Vanilla Ice Cream (page 112) for serving

Preheat the oven to 400°F/200°C/gas 6. In a small saucepan, melt the butter over medium-low heat and stir in the honey and wine. Cook until syrupy. Remove from heat and let cool slightly.

In a gratin dish, toss the apricots with the syrup and almonds. Roast, uncovered, for 20 minutes, or until the fruit is soft and the syrup is caramelized. Serve warm, over ice cream.

Vanilla Ice Cream | MAKES 1½ QT/1.4 L

2½ cups/600 ml heavy/double cream
2 cups/480 ml whole milk

2 vanilla beans/pods, halved lengthwise, or 2 tsp vanilla extract/essence
8 large egg yolks

¾ cup/150 g sugar
¼ tsp salt

In a medium saucepan, combine the cream and milk. Scrape the seeds from the vanilla beans, if using, and place the seeds and pods in the cream mixture. Cook over low heat for 5 minutes, or until bubbles form around the edges of the pan. Do not let simmer. Remove from heat. If using vanilla extract/essence, stir it into the mixture. Cover and let stand for 30 minutes. If using the vanilla bean/pod, remove the pod halves.

Using an electric mixer, beat the egg yolks, sugar, and salt at high speed until the mixture has doubled in volume. Reduce the speed to medium. Gradually beat in 1 cup/240 ml of the cream mixture to temper. Again add 1 cup/240 ml of the mixture and beat to combine. Return to the saucepan and cook over low heat, stirring often, until the mixture is thick enough to coat the back of a spoon, about 5 minutes. Remove from heat and strain into a medium bowl set in an ice bath. Let cool completely. Cover and refrigerate for at least 2 hours or overnight.

Freeze in an ice cream maker according to the manufacturer's instructions.

Weeknight Dinner

o o o

In the summer, we tend to get home from work and head directly out to the garden. Before we know it, everyone's starving and it's getting late. Here's a quick weeknight dinner that would also work for guests. Choose a dry but aromatic Sonoma Coast Riesling with the equally fragrant shrimp.

Haricots Verts, Goat Cheese, and Watermelon Salad ‖ SERVES 6

This is a cool salad recipe, perfect for the first really hot summer day. Haricots verts are the skinny French green beans, and their green color is gorgeous against the white of the goat cheese and the red of the watermelon. The trick to homegrown beans is to pick them early, while still very small and tender. At the market, choose the most slender beans you can find.

Watermelons take up a lot of real estate in the garden, so be forewarned. They'll send tendrils out to all corners, but their sweet juicy flesh is worth the encroachment!

The trick to making salads work with wine is to go easy on the acid, whether you're using citrus juice or vinegar. This fresh and lively salad is a fine accompaniment to grilled meat or fish. Riesling's bright acidity is perfect for this tangy salad.

¼ cup/60 ml extra-virgin olive oil

1 tbsp fresh lime juice

1 tsp balsamic vinegar

1 shallot, finely chopped

½ tsp salt

¼ tsp freshly ground pepper

1 lb/455 g haricots verts, trimmed

2 cups/340 g 1-in-/2.5-cm-cubed seedless watermelon

2 tbsp very thinly sliced fresh basil leaves

4 oz/115 g goat cheese, crumbled

In a small bowl, whisk together the oil, lime juice, vinegar, shallot, salt, and pepper. Let stand for at least 15 minutes, so the shallot can marinate.

In a large pot of salted boiling water, cook the beans for 4 to 5 minutes, or until crisp-tender. Drain and transfer to an ice water bath until cool; drain again and transfer to a large bowl. Add the watermelon, basil, and dressing. Toss to coat.

Divide among salad plates. Top each salad with goat cheese.

Grilled Coriander Shrimp Kabobs with Raita ‖ SERVES 6

I made these shrimp kabobs one warm summer night for our friends and their teenage son, Charlie. He and my six-year-old, Brian, polished off half a dozen skewers each, despite the sophisticated flavors of coriander, cumin, and cilantro, which proves that these kabobs will please almost anyone!

This simple and delicious main course could also serve 10 to 12 as an appetizer. The raita makes a terrific sauce not only for the shrimp, but for any kind of fish and even chicken. The sultry spices of this dish pair perfectly with an aromatic Riesling.

2 lb/910 g large shrimp/prawns, peeled and deveined, tails intact

MARINADE
¼ cup/60 g extra-virgin olive oil
2 tbsp fresh lime juice
1 tbsp ground coriander
1 tbsp ground cumin

2 tbsp chopped fresh cilantro/ fresh coriander
1 tsp salt
½ tsp freshly ground pepper

Raita (recipe follows) for serving

In a large bowl, combine the shrimp/prawns and all the marinade ingredients; stir well. Cover and refrigerate for at least 1 hour or up to 3 hours.

Soak 12 wooden skewers in water for 1 hour. Preheat a gas grill/barbecue to medium-high heat, or prepare a medium-hot fire in a charcoal grill/barbecue.

Thread 4 or 5 shrimp/prawns onto each skewer, threading through the top and bottom of each shrimp so it lies flat. Grill for 2 to 3 minutes on each side, or until evenly pink. Serve with the raita alongside for dipping.

Raita ‖ MAKES 2½ CUPS/600 ML

1½ cups/360 ml plain whole-milk yogurt
½ small shallot, finely chopped

1 cup/140 g finely diced peeled cucumber
2 tbsp finely chopped fresh mint

1 tsp salt
½ tsp freshly ground pepper

In a small bowl, combine all the ingredients and stir to blend.

Saffron and Pine Nut Couscous ||

This is my foolproof side dish; more interesting than rice, it takes less than ten minutes to make. The shallot and chicken stock add a depth of flavor to the couscous, and the bit of saffron lends some exoticism.

2 tbsp pine nuts

2 cups/480 ml chicken stock

1 tbsp extra-virgin olive oil

1 shallot, finely chopped

1½ cups/255 g couscous

Pinch of saffron threads

Preheat the oven to 350°F/180°C/gas 4. In a pie pan, spread the pine nuts in a single layer. Toast for 10 minutes, or until golden brown. Remove from the oven, pour into a bowl, and let cool.

In a small saucepan, bring the chicken stock to a low simmer. In a medium saucepan, heat the olive oil until shimmering. Add the shallot and sauté until translucent, about 3 minutes. Add the couscous and toss to coat. Add the saffron, chicken stock, and toasted pine nuts. Turn off the heat, cover, and steam for 5 minutes. Fluff with a fork and serve.

Sugared Icebox Plums with Basil || SERVES 6

This recipe is an ode to Luther Burbank, who first cultivated Santa Rosa plums here in Sonoma County more than a century ago. It also honors William Carlos Williams, who wrote about chilled plums in his famous poem, "This Is Just to Say." On a hot summer night, there's nothing better than cold, ripe summer fruit. This recipe combines plum slices with fresh basil and sugar. We fill big bowlfuls and sit out and look at the stars.

8 to 10 Santa Rosa plums, halved lengthwise and pitted
2 tbsp sugar

1 tbsp fresh lemon juice
2 tbsp very finely sliced fresh basil leaves

Cut each plum half lengthwise into quarters and put in a medium bowl. Add the sugar and lemon juice and toss to coat. Let stand for 20 minutes until the juices are released. Cover and refrigerate for at least 1 hour or up to 4 hours.

Remove the plums from the refrigerator and toss with the basil. Divide among bowls to serve.

Fall

Fall is my favorite time of year in wine country. It's time to harvest, and we've worked hard all year to get to this point. We've meticulously pruned our vines in the winter, waited with anticipation for the first shoots to appear in the spring, and worried over the baby shoots during frosty spring nights. After the spring frosts subside, we tie and train our growing shoots, giving them room to spread out and flourish on the trellises. We nurture the soil bed with compost and cover crops, irrigate, and watch the clusters swell and sweeten until they're ready to harvest.

When the first Champagne grapes are harvested in August, it makes front-page news in our local papers. And then we're off to the races. Sauvignon Blanc comes in next, followed by the other whites, and then the reds begin to come, too—thin-skinned Pinot Noir and Zinfandel. Soon, the roads and highways are chockablock with grape trucks, from big-rig flatbeds stacked with two-ton gondolas on their way to corporate wineries to pickups with loads of grapes destined for home winemakers' garages.

The smell of fermenting juice is everywhere in the valley, and the grape trucks rumble day and night. By late October, most of our grapes are off the vines, and the fermented juice has been pressed off and barreled down. A few weeks after the grapes are harvested, the vine leaves turn from green to yellow and begin to drop, liquid-ambar trees turn their glorious orange, and the indige-nous toyon fruits out its berries. The crackle of dry oak leaves is underfoot, and an electric current is in the air. Where before we prayed for sunny skies, now we pray for rain to moisten the dusty earth, which has seen no rain since spring. The golden hills, with their parched grass, and our anemic gardens long for a nice, long soak. The first rain comes and almost seems to evaporate. But then the rain comes in earnest, for days at a time, filling up the dry creek beds and rivers, creating standing puddles, and making everything green again. The temperature drops a bit, and we finally move inside, making the first tentative fire of the year, braising on the stove and giving the grill a rest after its long workout.

Those first rainy days are heaven for me. I'm released from my usual garden chores, and free to spend the day in my kitchen, where my menus get a little more complicated given the gift of time.

My palate changes as much for wine as for food. To match the braises and lush fall flavors, I move from summery Sauvignon Blanc to richer Chardonnay, and the warmth of a glass of red wine on a rainy day is a pleasure indeed.

The farmers' market now teems with pale baby turnips, orange persimmons, and crimson pomegranates. Piles of pears and apples beckon, and we make the first of many winter squash soups. Earthy mushrooms come after the first rain, awaiting shallots, butter, and cream to bring out their aromatic richness. Zinnias and marigolds provide our autumn color, and our rosebushes push on until after Thanksgiving, giving us beautiful rosehips to adorn our holiday tables. Fall is a rich time for entertaining.

The Fall Garden

The wine country garden in fall is a hybrid of still-producing late-summer vegetables, alongside the earliest seedlings planted for the winter garden. Tomato plants soldier on, even after the first rain, ripening more slowly. Cucumbers give their last gasp, their leaves turning yellow. Summer squash continues its relentless output, though most gardeners finally pull them up to make way for their winter gardens, having exhausted every recipe for zucchini known to man. Besides, the winter squash planted so long ago begins to turn orange on the vine, and we welcome the sweetness of butternut and acorn, Hub-bard, and Delicata into our kitchen. Root vegetables like

turnips, parsnips, and beets are ready to harvest and store for winter meals. The fig trees set their second crop, and pears and the last of the apples, made even sweeter by the cool weather, are ready to pick. The persimmon tree loses its leaves, and the fruit begins to turn fiery orange, awaiting its role in a crunchy salad or a sweet and spicy dessert. Fall's cooler weather makes for happy lettuces, and our pomegranate tree is laden with crimson orbs, the seeds staining hands and cutting boards.

We unearth seed packets of winter greens, making easy furrows in soil newly moistened by the first rain. We venture to our local nursery to find interesting seedlings of kale, broccoli rabe, and cauliflower. And finally, well into November, it's time to pull out the tomato plants, the cucumbers, and the squash. The winter garden is truly a pleasure; irrigation takes care of itself, with our abundant late fall and winter rains, and weeds are controlled by the cold temperatures. We pull on our garden boots only occasionally to meander out into the garden to cut some kale for a braise, or pull up a carrot or two for a mirepoix.

ASK THE WINEMAKER

How do you know when to harvest the grapes?

Winemaking is both an art and a science, as is perfectly demonstrated by the question of when to pick grapes. We determine when to harvest grapes with both technical and subjective information. Once August hits, we begin to sample our white grapes, using our sense of taste as well as an instrument called a refractometer, which measures the sugar content in the grapes by degrees of Brix. Named after nineteenth-century German chemist A. F. W. Brix, this system measures the percentage of solids in a given weight of juice. As a grape ripens, it dehydrates, leaving heavier solids and thus a higher Brix measurement. Sugar converts to alcohol during fermentation, so the higher the Brix, the higher the alcohol. White wines generally have lower alcohol than reds, so we pick them at lower sugars. We aim for 23° to 25° Brix in whites, and 24° to 28° in reds.

But Brix isn't the only measurement we use. The more subjective data of appearance and taste play a large part in determining when to pick grapes. First, we look at the berries to see if they're soft. Then we taste. As the grape ripens, green or herbaceous flavors should dissipate. The seeds in the grape should turn from green to brown. Green seeds impart astringency in the resulting wine. If we have sweet fruit flavors, the seeds are brown, and the Brix measurement is within an acceptable range, we're ready to pick.

In general, harvest begins in August and can extend into November. Grapes for sparkling wine come in first, in the second half of August, as they're deliberately picked at lower sugar levels than for still wine. Whites come in next, then thin-skinned red grapes like Pinot Noir and Zinfandel, and finally the thicker-skinned varieties like Merlot and Cabernet Sauvignon.

Harvest Picnic in the Vineyard

∘ ∘ ∘

Green Zebra Tomato, White Corn, and Mozzarella Salad / 127

Pan-Seared Five-Spice Duck Breast with Balsamic Jus / 128

French Lentil, Prosciutto, and Pepper Salad / 130

Sautéed Romano Beans with Shallots, Pine Nuts, and Mint / 131

Kadota Fig Tart with Mascarpone Cream / 133

We started doing a harvest lunch in October a couple of years ago. Now, it just wouldn't be harvest without it. We invite our wine club members, friends of the winery, our distributors, the Hanna family, and the winery staff. We serve our lunch just outside the cellar doors, but the menu is lovely for a picnic, too. The wines for this menu should be rustic and plentiful. Serve Russian River Valley Chardonnay for a starter white, as its richness is just right for the cooler fall weather. And an earthy Russian River Pinot Noir is the perfect weight to pair with the duck. Since the harvest season is truly a special occasion, serve a dessert wine like Moscato to go with the fig tart.

Green Zebra Tomato, White Corn, and Mozzarella Salad || SERVES 6

Green Zebra tomatoes are the striped variety. My kids get a huge kick out of them, and they are gorgeous when sliced crosswise. This salad is not only colorful, but makes great use of fall's last tomatoes and corn. Seek out fresh mozzarella for this recipe. The supermarket variety looks and tastes like rubber. If you can't find fresh mozzarella, you are better off substituting another artisan cheese, such as Taleggio or Crescenza.

Chardonnay will taste great with this salad, particularly with the richness of the cheese. Just make sure the wine isn't too oaky.

2 cups/340 g white corn kernels (about 3 ears)

¼ cup/60 ml extra-virgin olive oil, plus more for drizzling

1 tbsp balsamic vinegar

1 tbsp red wine vinegar

½ tsp salt, plus more for sprinkling

¼ tsp freshly ground pepper, plus more for sprinkling

2 cups/55 g arugula/rocket

6 small Green Zebra or other heirloom tomatoes, quartered

1 ball fresh mozzarella, cut into slices 1 in/2.5 cm thick

In a covered steamer over simmering water, steam the corn until crisp-tender, about 5 minutes. Remove from the steamer and set aside.

In a small bowl, whisk together the ¼ cup/60 ml oil, the vinegars, the ½ tsp salt, and the ¼ tsp pepper. In a large bowl, toss the corn, arugula/rocket, and tomatoes with the vinaigrette and then arrange on a platter. Add the mozzarella and drizzle with olive oil. Sprinkle with salt and pepper.

Pan-Seared Five-Spice Duck Breast with Balsamic Jus || SERVES 6

The first time I made duck, I prepared traditional Peking duck using two enormous birds special-ordered from the butcher. After three days of painstaking preparation, every surface of my kitchen was covered in duck fat, and the ducks had shrunk down so much I only had a few ounces of meat to serve the six people walking through my door for dinner.

Duck breasts are the answer! You can find them in the freezer section of your market if you can't find fresh, or you can special-order them from your butcher. They're much less fatty than duck legs or thighs, and they don't shrink much at all. In this recipe, the sear on high heat gets the skin nice and crispy. Aromatic five-spice powder gives the duck an exotic flair. An easy pan sauce results from deglazing the pan with wine and balsamic vinegar.

Duck and Pinot Noir are meant for each other. An elegant Russian River Valley Pinot Noir is a perfect match, and stands up to the aromatic spice rub.

1 large garlic clove, finely chopped

1 tbsp grated peeled fresh ginger

2 tsp five-spice powder

1 tsp salt

½ tsp freshly ground pepper

4 single duck breasts

1 tbsp extra-virgin olive oil

¼ cup/60 ml dry red wine

2 tbsp balsamic vinegar

In a large, heavy self-sealing plastic bag, combine the garlic, ginger, five-spice powder, salt, and pepper. Add the duck breasts, seal, and refrigerate for at least 1 hour or up to 24 hours. Remove from the refrigerator 1 hour before cooking.

Preheat the oven to 400°F/200°C/gas 6. In a large oven-proof sauté pan, heat the olive oil over medium-high heat until shimmering. Sear the duck breast, skin side down, for 5 minutes; turn and sear for 5 minutes on the other side. Transfer the pan to the oven and roast for 5 minutes for

medium-rare. Transfer the duck breasts to a plate and keep warm.

To make a balsamic jus, pour off the fat from the pan. Return the pan to medium-high heat, add the wine, and stir to scrape up the browned bits from the bottom of the pan. Cook to reduce the wine by half. Add the balsamic vinegar and cook to reduce for several more minutes.

Cut the duck breasts into diagonal slices and serve drizzled with the balsamic jus.

French Lentil, Prosciutto, and Pepper Salad || SERVES 6 TO 8

I adore lentils, particularly the green French variety, as well as the little black ones, sometimes known as beluga lentils because of their resemblance to caviar. Both of these types hold their shape better than the typical brown lentil, and their nutty texture and flavor are divine. This is my favorite fall salad, made a bit indulgent with the addition of prosciutto. I first made this for an autumnal baby shower, and it was a major hit. The earthiness of the lentils and prosciutto plays wonderfully off the color and sweetness of autumn's bounty of peppers. This salad works equally well with meat, chicken, or fish. Best of all, it can be served at room temperature, and tastes even better the next day. So, make the salad the day before, heat up the grill, pop a few corks, and enjoy the sunshine!

Serve this earthy salad alongside the duck breasts with a glass of Russian River Pinot Noir.

⅓ cup/75 ml extra-virgin olive oil, plus 1 tbsp

6 paper-thin slices prosciutto di Parma, finely chopped

2 shallots, finely chopped

½ cup/140 g finely diced carrots

½ cup/140 g finely diced red bell pepper/capsicum

2 cups/400 g green French lentils, rinsed and drained

¼ cup/10 g finely chopped fresh flat-leaf parsley

2 tsp finely chopped fresh thyme

2 tbsp red wine vinegar

1 tbsp Dijon mustard

½ tsp salt

¼ tsp freshly ground pepper

In a medium sauté pan or frying pan, heat the 1 tbsp olive oil over medium heat until shimmering. Add the prosciutto and sauté until lightly browned, about 5 minutes. Add the shallots and sauté until translucent, about 3 minutes. Add the carrots and bell pepper/capsicum and sauté for 5 minutes, or until crisp-tender. Set aside.

In a medium saucepan, combine the lentils with at least 4 cups/960 ml salted water. Bring to a boil, then reduce to a simmer, cover, and cook until the lentils are just tender, about 30 minutes. Drain, then transfer to a large bowl. Add the prosciutto mixture, along with the parsley and thyme; toss to combine.

In a small bowl, whisk together the vinegar and mustard. Gradually whisk in the ⅓ cup/75 ml olive oil until emulsified. Add the salt and pepper. Toss the lentil salad with the dressing. Taste and adjust the seasoning.

Sautéed Romano Beans with Shallots, Pine Nuts, and Mint || SERVES 6

I've learned that some ingredient additions can go a long way. These beans really sing with the rich crunch of pine nuts and the fresh surprise of mint.

Romano beans are a flat Italian pole bean variety, but feel free to use yellow wax beans if you can't find Romanos. Pole beans are easy to grow in the garden, as long as you pick them before they grow too old and starchy.

2 tbsp pine nuts

1 lb/455 g Romano beans, trimmed

1 tbsp extra-virgin olive oil

2 shallots, finely chopped

1 garlic clove, finely chopped

1 tbsp finely chopped fresh mint

1 tsp salt

½ tsp freshly ground pepper

Preheat the oven to 350°F/180°C/gas 4. Spread the pine nuts in a pie pan and bake until golden, about 10 minutes.

In a large pot of salted boiling water, cook the beans for 3 minutes, or until crisp-tender. Transfer to an ice water bath until cool. Drain and set aside.

In a large sauté pan or frying pan, heat the olive oil over medium heat until shimmering. Add the shallots and sauté until translucent, about 3 minutes. Add the garlic and sauté for 1 minute. Add the beans and sauté until heated through. Add the pine nuts, mint, salt, and pepper. Toss to coat.

Kadota Fig Tart with Mascarpone Cream ‖ SERVES 6 TO 8

Three fig trees grow in my garden, including a green Kadota variety whose branches I can see from my dining room window. In five years, this tree has grown twice as big as the other two, and its fruit is sweet, luxuriant, and plentiful, yielding one crop in late summer and another one, smaller and sweeter, in the fall.

This tart works with whatever fresh fruit is in season. I love it with summer raspberries, but in the fall, delicate and honeyed Kadota figs are perfect. If you can't find them, Black Mission figs can be substituted. Accompany the tart with a slightly effervescent Moscato for a festive ending to a harvest lunch.

PASTRY DOUGH

1½ cups/320 g all-purpose/plain flour

¼ tsp salt

½ cup/115 g cold unsalted butter, cut into chunks

3 tbsp ice water

FILLING

8 oz/225 g mascarpone cheese

⅓ cup/75 ml sour cream

⅓ cup/75 ml honey

1 tsp salt

8 Kadota figs, quartered lengthwise

Honey for drizzling

For the pastry: In a food processor, pulse the flour and salt until combined. Add the butter and process until the mixture forms coarse crumbs. Add the ice water, 1 tbsp at a time, until the mixture begins to come together. Transfer the dough to a floured surface and form into a disk. Wrap in plastic wrap and refrigerate for at least 30 minutes or up to 2 days.

To make the tart shell, remove the dough from refrigerator and allow to soften for a few minutes. Roll into an 11-in/28-cm round. Fit the dough into a 9-in/23-cm fluted tart pan/flan tin with a removable bottom, pressing the dough into the sides of the pan. Run the rolling pin over the top of the pan to trim the dough flush with the rim. Refrigerate for at least 30 minutes or up to 24 hours.

continued

Adjust an oven rack in the center of the oven and preheat the oven to 375°F/190°C/gas 5. Remove the crust from the refrigerator and prick the pastry all over with a fork. Line the crust with parchment/baking paper and fill with pie weights or dried beans. Bake for 20 minutes. Remove the paper and weights and bake for 5 to 10 minutes more, or until just golden. Transfer to a wire rack/cake cooler and let cool completely.

For the filling: In a medium bowl, whisk together the mascarpone, sour cream, the ⅓ cup/75 ml honey, and the salt. Using a rubber spatula, spread the mascarpone mixture evenly in the crust. Arrange the figs in concentric circles on top of the mascarpone mixture. Drizzle with additional honey. Remove the sides of the pan and cut the tart into wedges to serve.

ASK THE WINEMAKER

What are sulfites?

Sulfur dioxide, also known as sulfites, is a preservative and antioxidant widely used in wine. It's also used to preserve some dried fruits. In winemaking, yeast naturally produces sulfites during fermentation. Extra sulfites are added to most wines, whether white or red. Sulfites keep white wines from oxidizing, and preserve their bright aromas and flavors. Red wines contain tannin from their extended contact with grape skins. Tannin is a preservative, so red wines need less sulfite than whites, but some is needed to prevent premature aging and keep bacteria at bay. Sulfites also keep wine barrels from harboring acetic bacteria, which can turn the contents of a wine barrel into vinegar.

In the United States, wines must state "contains sulfites" on their labels if they include 10 ppm or more.

Sulfites can shut down the aromatics on some varieties, like Pinot Noir, so we add judiciously. The Food and Drug Administration estimates that only 1 percent of the population is allergic to sulfites. Symptoms include skin rashes and itchiness, along with respiratory difficulty.

There is no evidence that sulfites cause headaches. The most likely culprits are dehydration and too much wine. Drinking a glass of water for each glass of wine usually resolves this problem. Most people who get headaches from wine do so from red wine rather than white. Red wines contain significantly fewer sulfites than white wines, so the histamines in red wine may be a culprit.

Autumn Dinner

○ ○ ○

Spicy Eggplant Caviar with Pita Crisps / 137

Fall Lettuces with Pear and Pecorino / 140

Pan-Seared Hanger Steak with Porcini-Merlot Reduction / 141

Roasted Potatoes and Shallots with Herbed Aioli / 142

Pear Tarte Tatin with Ginger Ice Cream / 143

September can be one of the warmest times of the year in wine country. But the evenings are cool, and red meat sounds good again. Here's a lovely casual dinner party that elevates everyday steak and potatoes. I like to up the ante and serve this menu with pedigreed wines, pairing a sparkling wine with the eggplant caviar, then pouring the best Sonoma or Napa Cabernet Sauvignon I can muster.

Spicy Eggplant Caviar with Pita Crisps || SERVES 6

I usually plant four or five varieties of eggplant/aubergines a year, from the slender Asian varieties to the larger globes, in a rainbow of colors ranging from creamy white to vermilion to the deepest purple. This vegetable is practically its own food group in Mediterranean cuisine, and is fantastic for food and wine pairing, as its rich flesh and creamy texture work with both white and red wines.

If your eggplant/aubergine has a lot of large seeds, remove them after roasting. Sun Gold tomatoes add sweetness and vibrant color to the dip, and parsley adds a fresh component.

A sparkling wine from Mendocino is a nice surprise with this creamy dish, and a good companion to the crisp pitas.

1 globe eggplant/aubergine, halved lengthwise

1 small garlic clove, finely chopped

½ tsp ground cumin

8 Sun Gold cherry tomatoes, halved, or regular cherry tomatoes, quartered

1 tsp finely chopped fresh flat-leaf parsley

½ tsp salt

¼ tsp freshly ground pepper

1 tbsp extra-virgin olive oil

Pita Crisps (page 139) for serving

Preheat the oven to 400°F/200°C/gas 6. Generously oil a baking sheet/tray. Place the eggplant/aubergine, cut side down, on the prepared pan and roast until soft, about 45 minutes. Remove from the oven, let cool, and peel off the skin. Finely chop the eggplant/aubergine and transfer to a medium bowl. Add the garlic, cumin, tomatoes, parsley, salt, pepper, and olive oil and stir gently to combine. Transfer to a serving bowl and serve, accompanied with the pita crisps.

Pita Crisps || MAKES 48 CRISPS

3 pita breads (or Syrian Pita, page 109)
2 tbsp extra-virgin olive oil

1 small garlic clove, finely chopped
¼ tsp salt

⅛ tsp freshly ground pepper

Preheat the oven to 350°F/180°C/gas 4. Separate the pitas horizontally into two rounds, then stack and cut into 8 wedges. Place the pita wedges in a single layer on a baking sheet/tray. In a small bowl, whisk together the olive oil, garlic, salt, and pepper. Brush the wedges with the garlic oil. Bake for 10 minutes, or until crisp and golden brown. Remove to a wire rack/cake cooler and let cool.

Fall Lettuces
with Pear and Pecorino ‖ SERVES 6

Fall is a terrific time to harvest lettuce from your garden. The trick is to
sow the seeds in August, so you have tender lettuces in the fall. In my
garden, lettuce bolts in the height of the summer, particularly those lovely
delicate-leaved varieties. Once the cooler nights of fall hit and the days
grow a little shorter, lettuce returns heroically. I like to use the red-leafed
varieties in the fall because the color is so autumnal. Good fall lettuce
varieties to grow are Flame, Firecracker, Lolla Rossa, and Speckled.

Pears are everywhere in the fall; the first are harvested east of us in
Lake County, then local pears arrive in late August and September. If
you're making this salad ahead of time, submerge the pears in lemon-
spiked water to prevent browning until you're ready to toss the salad.
Drain and add the pears to the salad at the last minute.

Many recipes combine pears and a blue cheese like Gorgonzola.
For a more delicate salad, I like to play the nutty saltiness of pecorino
against the sweetness of the pears.

A coastal Chardonnay, with its aroma and flavor of ripe pear, is
a fine companion for this salad.

¼ cup/60 ml extra-virgin olive oil

1 tbsp red wine vinegar

1 tsp balsamic vinegar

½ tsp salt

¼ tsp freshly ground pepper

Leaves from 1 small head red-leafed
lettuce, torn

1 red, Bosc, or Anjou pear, halved
lengthwise, cored, and cut into
1-in/2.5-cm lengthwise slices

2-oz/55-g chunk pecorino cheese

In a small bowl, whisk together the oil, vinegars, salt,
and pepper. In a large salad bowl, combine the lettuce
leaves, pear, and vinaigrette. Toss gently and divide
among 6 plates. Using a vegetable peeler, shave curls
of pecorino onto each salad.

Pan-Seared Hanger Steak with Porcini-Merlot Reduction || SERVES 6

I'm having a love affair with hanger steak. I started ordering it in restaurants a couple of years ago, and then it began to occasionally show up in high-end grocery stores. Now it's a regular at the meat counter of my local market. Hanger steak is cut from the area between the last rib and the loin. Previously called the butcher tenderloin, it's very juicy and tender, with the added benefit of being considerably less expensive than pricey cuts like filet.

Fall is mushroom season, so they take pride of place alongside the steak. Feel free to use whatever mushroom you find at your market. On the north coast, we begin seeing porcini and chanterelles soon after the first good rain of the fall. But shiitakes are a nice substitute, and readily available at the market, as are cremini.

Steak and Cabernet are meant for each other, so serve a classic Napa or Sonoma Cabernet Sauvignon here.

1 tbsp extra-virgin olive oil

One 1½- to 2-lb/680- to 910-g hanger steak, cut into 6 portions

Salt and freshly ground pepper

4 oz/115 g porcini or stemmed shiitake mushrooms, or 8 oz/225 g cremini/brown mushrooms, brushed clean and thinly sliced

2 garlic cloves, finely chopped

½ cup/120 ml Merlot

¼ cup/60 ml good-quality beef stock

In a large, heavy sauté pan or frying pan, heat the oil over medium-high heat until shimmering. Season the hanger steaks on both sides with salt and pepper, then sear in the hot oil until browned, about 2 minutes per side. Transfer to a plate.

Add the mushrooms to the pan and return to medium-high heat. Add the garlic and stir to combine. Add half of the wine and cook the mushrooms for 2 to 3 minutes. Add the remaining wine and the beef stock. Return the steaks to the pan, cover, and cook for 2½ minutes on each side for medium-rare. Add salt and pepper to taste.

Serve the steaks drizzled with the pan sauce.

Roasted Potatoes and Shallots with Herbed Aioli ‖ SERVES 6

There's something so comforting about a roasted potato, especially when combined with the sweetness of roasted shallots. This delicious side dish can be served warm or at room temperature. Any small potato will do here, including the fingerling varieties, which should be cut in half lengthwise to highlight their interesting shape.

2 lb/910 g small red or Yukon Gold potatoes, or a combination, halved

12 shallots, peeled

2 tbsp extra-virgin olive oil

1 tsp salt

½ tsp freshly ground pepper

HERBED AIOLI

3 garlic cloves, finely chopped

2 large egg yolks

Juice of 1 lemon

2 tbsp finely chopped mixed fresh herbs, such as chives, oregano, rosemary, and/or thyme

1 tsp salt

½ tsp freshly ground pepper

1 cup/240 ml extra-virgin olive oil

Preheat the oven to 400°F/200°C/gas 6. In a roasting pan/tray, toss the potatoes and shallots with the olive oil, salt, and pepper. Roast for 30 to 40 minutes, or until the potatoes are browned and the shallots are soft; remove from heat and keep warm. If the shallots are cooking more quickly than the potatoes, remove the shallots and return them at the end of cooking.

Meanwhile, for the aioli: In a food processor, combine the garlic, egg yolks, lemon juice, herbs, salt, and pepper. Pulse to combine. With the machine running, gradually add the olive oil until emulsified. Taste and adjust the seasoning.

Serve the potatoes and shallots with a spoonful of the aioli alongside.

Pear Tarte Tatin with Ginger Ice Cream | SERVES 6 TO 8

Tarte Tatin was the first grown-up dessert I mastered. After graduating from the ubiquitous cookie and brownie baking of my youth, I ventured into more unfamiliar territory. Now, I realize that baking is no more difficult than savory cooking, although you do need to be exact with your measurements. I like to make this tart first thing in the morning, so the wonderful caramel, ginger, and pear fragrances fill the house all day. Homemade ginger ice cream is the perfect accompaniment.

TART DOUGH

1¼ cups/160 g all-purpose/plain flour

¼ tsp salt

7 tbsp/100 g cold unsalted butter, cut into chunks

2 to 3 tbsp ice water

FILLING

6 tbsp/85 g unsalted butter

6 large Anjou pears, peeled, quartered, and cored

½ cup/100 g sugar

1 tbsp grated peeled fresh ginger

Ginger Ice Cream (page 144) for serving

For the dough: In a food processor, pulse the flour and salt until blended. Add the butter and pulse until the mixture resembles coarse crumbs. Add 2 tbsp of the ice water and pulse. If the mixture doesn't begin to hold together, add 1 more tbsp ice water. Do not let the dough form a ball, or it will be overworked and tough. On a floured surface, form the dough into a ball, then a disk. Wrap in plastic wrap and refrigerate for at least 1 hour or up to 2 days.

Adjust an oven rack in the center of the oven. Preheat the oven to 425°F/220°C/gas 7.

For the filling: Melt the butter in a large sauté pan over medium-high heat until foaming. Reduce the heat to medium; add the pears, sugar, and ginger and stir to combine. Cook for 20 minutes, stirring occasionally so the pears do not stick. Increase the heat to medium-high and allow the pears to brown nicely, another 10 to 15 minutes.

Pile the pear mixture into an unbuttered 9-in/23-cm tarte Tatin pan or frying pan.

On a floured surface, roll the dough into an 11-in/28-cm round. Place the pastry on top of the pear mixture, tucking the pastry down inside the edges of the pan.

Bake the tart for 40 minutes, or until golden brown. Remove from the oven and place a flat plate on top of the pan. Invert the pan and give the bottom a few taps to release any stuck fruit. Serve with ginger ice cream.

Ginger Ice Cream | MAKES 1½ QT/1.4 L

2½ cups/600 ml heavy/double cream

2 cups/480 ml whole milk

¼ cup lightly packed grated peeled fresh ginger

2 tsp ground ginger

8 large egg yolks

¾ cup/150 g sugar

¼ tsp salt

In a medium saucepan, combine the cream, milk, and fresh ginger. Cook over low heat for 5 minutes, or until bubbles form around the edges of the pan. Do not simmer. Remove from heat, whisk in the ground ginger, cover, and let stand for 30 minutes.

Using an electric mixer, beat the egg yolks, sugar, and salt at high speed until the mixture has doubled in volume. Reduce the speed to medium. Gradually beat in 1 cup/240 ml of the cream mixture to temper. Again add 1 cup/240 ml of the mixture and beat to combine. Return to the saucepan and cook over low heat, stirring often, until the mixture is thick enough to coat the back of a spoon, about 5 minutes. Remove from heat and strain into a medium bowl set in an ice bath. Let cool completely. Cover and refrigerate for at least 2 hours or overnight.

Freeze in an ice cream maker according to the manufacturer's instructions.

ASK THE WINEMAKER

What are organic wines?

For a wine to be labeled "certified organic," the grapes must be grown according to organic standards set by the USDA, which means no pesticides, herbicides, fungicides, chemical fertilizers, or synthetic chemicals may be used on the vines or in the soil. The wine must also be produced and bottled in a certified organic facility, with no added sulfites.

While many wineries farm their grapes organically, the biggest stumbling block to organic certification is not being able to add sulfites to the wine to preserve color and flavor. Many winemakers forgo organic certification in order to ensure a quality product with some longevity, so you might see a label that states "made with organic grapes" rather than "organic wine."

Organic wines grew at a rate of 18 percent last year, still far below the rise in certified organic foods. Consumers report uneven quality in organic wines, though those committed to organics are willing to take the risk in order to find organic producers they can trust.

Weeknight Dinner

○ ○ ○

Lolla Rossa, Fig, and Feta Salad / 148

Creamy Herbed Orzo / 149

Cumin-Crusted Grilled Pork Tenderloin with Salsa Verde / 151

Grilled Sweet and Hot Peppers / 152

Chocolate Chip, Dried Cherry, and Pistachio Cookies / 154

Here's a foolproof fall dinner. We all need a delicious and quick menu for weeknights when the temptation is high to just order a pizza. Since they don't deliver out to the country, I've devised a series of seasonal menus that are quick to prepare after a long day at work. In this fall menu, the pork rub can be put on right before you grill, and the tenderloin cooks in ten minutes. You can grill the peppers right alongside the tenderloin. The orzo, once cooked, takes seconds to assemble.

Sauvignon Blanc is a tangy match for the feta in the salad. Pork and Pinot Noir are best partners.

Lolla Rossa, Fig, and Feta Salad || SERVES 6

Lolla Rossa is a beautiful crimson-leaved salad green that grows in our garden and can be found at farmers' markets in the fall. Any red-leafed lettuce would be a fine substitute. Our Mission fig tree is prolific with its second crop, offering up the sweetest, most succulent figs. I love them in this quintessential fall salad.

The winey flavor of the figs, along with the salty feta and crunch of the walnuts, makes this a salad to enjoy with either Sauvignon Blanc or Pinot Noir.

¼ cup/30 g walnuts, coarsely chopped

¼ cup/60 ml extra-virgin olive oil

1 tsp red wine vinegar

1 tbsp balsamic vinegar

½ tsp salt

¼ tsp freshly ground pepper

Leaves from 2 small heads Lolla Rossa lettuce, or 1 head other red-leafed lettuce

½ cup/70 g crumbled feta cheese

6 small Mission or Kabota figs, quartered

Preheat the oven to 350°F/180°C/gas 4. Spread the walnuts in a pie pan. Toast in the oven for 10 minutes, or until fragrant.

In a small bowl, whisk together the oil, vinegars, salt, and pepper. In a salad bowl, toss the lettuce and walnuts with the vinaigrette to coat well. Add the feta and figs and toss gently. Divide among plates and serve.

Creamy Herbed Orzo ‖ SERVES 6

This dish is so easy, my six-year-old son, Brian, can make it. The heat of the drained pasta melts the creamy ricotta, made fresh with bright green herbs. It's a perfect, quick weeknight side dish when everyone is starving and can't wait an hour for dinner.

2 cups/400 g orzo pasta

1 cup/225 g fresh whole-milk ricotta

1 heaping tbsp finely chopped fresh flat-leaf parsley

1 tbsp finely chopped fresh chives

1 tsp salt

½ tsp freshly ground pepper

In a large pot of salted boiling water, cook the orzo for 8 to 10 minutes, or until al dente. Drain and transfer to a bowl. Add the ricotta, herbs, salt, and pepper. Toss to coat and serve at once.

Cumin-Crusted Grilled Pork Tenderloin with Salsa Verde || SERVES 6

I teach this recipe in my cooking classes because it's easy and delicious. Pork tenderloin marinates and grills quickly, and slices up beautifully on the plate. The key is to sear it first, and not to overcook it. The cumin in the marinade for this dish adds an earthiness that really comes out on the grill.

A medium-bodied Pinot Noir from Carneros, Russian River Valley, or Oregon is a fine match with the aromatic pork.

4 garlic cloves, finely chopped

2 tbsp ground cumin

1 tsp ground coriander

2 tbsp extra-virgin olive oil

1 tsp dry mustard

1 tbsp salt

½ tsp freshly ground pepper

2 pork tenderloins

Salsa Verde (page 79) for serving

In a large, heavy self-sealing plastic bag, combine the garlic, spices, olive oil, dry mustard, salt, and pepper. Add the pork, turn to coat, and refrigerate for at least 2 hours or overnight.

Preheat a gas grill/barbecue to medium-high, or prepare a medium-hot fire in a charcoal grill/barbecue.

Remove the pork from the refrigerator 30 minutes before grilling. Grill the pork for 3 minutes on each of all four sides, a total of 12 minutes. Transfer to a carving board and tent with aluminum foil; let rest for 10 to 15 minutes. Cut the pork into slices 1 in/2.5 cm thick; reserve the juices. Serve drizzled with the juices and Salsa Verde.

Grilled Sweet and Hot Peppers   ‖   SERVES 6

The last of the bell peppers/capsicums appear in late fall. They grow prolifically in the garden, their jewel tones hidden beneath dark green foliage. The yellow and purple and fiery orange flesh brightens any plate. But there are also other varieties of sweet peppers. Here a mixture of peppers and chiles is simply grilled, then tossed with salt and pepper.

Sauvignon Blanc can stand up to the heat of the chiles in this recipe.

3 bell peppers/capsicums, either red, orange, yellow, purple or a combination, stemmed, seeded, and deveined

2 banana or gypsy peppers, stemmed, seeded, and deveined

3 small chiles, such as serrano or jalapeño, halved, seeded, and deveined

2 tbsp extra-virgin olive oil

½ tsp salt

¼ tsp freshly ground pepper

Preheat a gas grill/barbecue to medium-high, or prepare a medium-hot fire in a charcoal grill/barbecue.

Cut the bell peppers/capsicums and banana peppers into lengthwise slices 2 in/12 mm wide. In a medium bowl, toss the peppers and chiles with the olive oil, salt, and pepper. Grill for 3 to 5 minutes on each side, or just until tender.

Chocolate Chip, Dried Cherry, and Pistachio Cookies | MAKES ABOUT 4 DOZEN COOKIES/BISCUITS

Yes, I know, it's too much to whip up a batch of cookies on a weeknight. We make them on the weekends, and after they cool, we place them in freezer bags and store them in the freezer, pulling a few out all week long for after-dinner treats. I like the rustic crumb given by the oatmeal. These cookies are elevated from the everyday by the tangy dried cherries and exotic pistachios.

1 cup/107 g old-fashioned rolled oats

1¾ cups/225 g all-purpose/plain flour

1 tsp baking soda/bicarbonate of soda

1 tsp salt

1 cup/115 g unsalted butter at room temperature

1 cup/200 g packed brown sugar/ Demerara sugar

½ cup/100 g granulated sugar

1 tsp vanilla extract/essence

2 large eggs

12 oz/340 g bittersweet chocolate, chopped

1 cup/115 g dried cherries

1 cup/115 g pistachio nuts, chopped

Adjust an oven rack in the center of the oven. Preheat the oven to 375°F/190°C/gas 5. In a food processor or blender, finely grind the oats. Sift the flour, ground oats, baking soda/bicarbonate of soda, and salt together into a medium bowl.

Using a stand mixer fitted with the paddle attachment, cream the butter and two sugars until light and fluffy. Add the vanilla and then the eggs, one at a time, stopping to scrape down the sides of the bowl once or twice. Add the flour mixture in two stages, mixing just to combine. Add the chocolate, cherries, and pistachios and stir by hand to blend.

Drop by rounded tablespoon onto ungreased baking sheets/trays. Bake for 10 minutes, or until golden brown. Transfer from the pan to a wire rack/cake cooler to cool. Store in sealable plastic bags for up to 2 days, or in the freezer for several weeks.

How should I stock my wine cellar?

If you are lucky enough to be collecting wine for a cellar, you are in store for some great fun. And remember, you don't have to spend a fortune to put together a wine cellar. There are options in all price ranges. Whether you have a full-fledged cellar, a cool basement, or a wine refrigerator capable of storing a fair amount of bottles, the same guidelines apply.

Invest in wines based on what each region does best. Breadth is more important than depth, and will ensure you end up with a cellar that's more than just Napa Cabernet. There are hundreds of choices, but here's a plan that you can supplement as your interest and pocketbook allow.

First, let's home in on the specialties in each wine region. Different regions generally do one thing well. That's not to say they don't produce other great wines, but in general a region is known for a particular wine because a specific grape grows particularly well there. In California, for example, the very cool Anderson Valley in Mendocino is famous for its sparkling wines.

Sparkling wines/Champagne: In general, you want to drink sparkling wines within a year or two of purchase. French Champagne ages beautifully because of its higher acidity, however, so add a bottle or two of that to round out the sparkling category.

White wines: Sonoma's cool Russian River Valley and New Zealand's Marlborough region have similar climates, and not surprisingly make great Sauvignon Blanc. Sauvignon is not made to age, so drink these wines within a year or two of purchase and replace with new vintages. If you're like me, you'll go through a lot of Sauvignon Blanc, particularly in the warmer months, so you might want to buy it by the case. Not a Sauvignon Blanc fan? A Pinot

Gris from Oregon or Alsace would check the zingy white wine box just as well.

A more medium-bodied white wine is next, which brings us to barrel-fermented Chardonnay. The Sonoma Coast and Carneros in California produce first-rate Chardonnay, but you'll find excellent-quality Chardonnay from areas on the Central Coast as well. A white Burgundy like a minerally Meursault would be a lovely French option, and would age five years or more. Don't like Chardonnay but want a lush white wine? Try a Viognier or a dry Riesling that has some barrel fermentation.

Red wines: We'll focus on lighter reds first, which brings us squarely to Pinot Noir, from Sonoma's Russian River Valley, Oregon's Willamette Valley, or, of course, the Gold Coast of Burgundy. The French wines will age quite a bit longer than the California and Oregon versions, so you can save them for five years or longer.

The Syrah/Shiraz category gives you a chance to try the same variety grown in two completely different countries (the terms *Syrah* and *Shiraz* refer to the same grape). I suggest a Syrah from the Rhône Valley in France and a Shiraz from Australia. Zinfandels from Paso Robles and from Sonoma's Dry Creek Valley are a must for any American wine drinker. Just be aware that they will not age forever, so drink them within five years or so of purchase.

The king of your cellar will be Cabernet Sauvignon, but do know that there are some wonderful, age-worthy Merlots out there with considerable heft, and due to oversupply, they are blissfully underpriced. Cabernet Sauvignon from Napa is the standard bearer for Cabs (with a corresponding kingly price tag). Do invest in these, but know that you have other great options for more everyday

continued

consumption. Sonoma's Alexander Valley makes fruit-forward, lush Cabernets that are great values. If you're a Cabernet lover, you might invest in some French Bordeaux to add breadth to your Cabernet selection. These wines do need aging, so store them for at least five years before you open them, and decant them when you do.

Once you've got these basics down, you can experiment with lesser-known varieties. A fan of Italy? Try Italian whites like Falanghina or Soave, or a red Aglianico from the Campania region. More well-known varieties like Soave, Sangiovese, and Valpolicella merit space in your cellar as well. Spain strike your fancy? A white Rueda, or a red Rioja or Tempranillo, would be a great addition.

As for dessert wines, choices abound from California, France, and, of course, Portugal. I always have a bottle of late-harvest Sauvignon Blanc, Sauternes, or Muscat on hand. Both tawny and ruby ports are great options for after dinner.

Finally, space allowing, you can add depth to your cellar by including more producers of your favorite varieties.

The best advice is to have fun, and don't forget what you have, especially the wines that don't age as well. There's nothing worse than pulling the cork on a wine forgotten for years in the cellar, only to find that it's completely over the hill. Keep your whites at eye level and try to restrain yourself from popping the corks on those expensive reds meant to be laid down.

Traditional Wine Country Thanksgiving

○ ○ ○

Arugula Salad with Fuyu Persimmons and Almonds / 158

Grill-Roasted Herbed Turkey with Chardonnay Gravy / 161

Winter Squash Gratin with Caramelized Onions, Chiles, and Thyme / 163

Brussels Sprouts Braised in White Wine with Pancetta / 164

Baby Turnips Braised in Sweet Butter / 165

Gravenstein Apple and Dried Cranberry Tart / 166

My family loves traditional Thanksgiving dinners. I confess I like a more adventurous menu that celebrates the bounty of late fall, so I've included a Mediterranean-inspired menu as well (page 169). Here are two wine country Thanksgiving menus that take advantage of late-fall produce. An aromatic dry Gewürztraminer from Anderson Valley or a zesty Napa or Sonoma Zinfandel works well with turkey.

Arugula Salad with Fuyu Persimmons and Almonds ‖ SERVES 6

There could not be a prettier fall salad than this one, which gets raves every time I make it. The peppery arugula contrasts with sweet persimmons and crunchy almonds. Persimmons ripen in late fall on sculptural branches that have already lost their leaves. Their stark beauty is a harbinger of the cold weather to come.

Persimmons are easy to grow and, for me, herald Thanksgiving. The more common Hachiya persimmon is larger and has a tapered globe-like shape. This variety of persimmon is very astringent unless fully ripe, so choose only those that are soft. Hachiyas are best used pureed for baking persimmon breads, cookies, and steamed puddings, or simply eating with a spoon.

Fuyu persimmons are smaller and look like a squat orange tomato. They are sweet and ripe when hard and crunchy, and are a lovely foil for spicy greens and nuts in salads. Their bright orange color and starburst centers make them a dramatic addition to the holiday table.

Chocolate persimmons, a more unusual variety, are starting to appear now, mostly in specialty grocery stores and farmers' markets. They have a tangy flavor and lovely dark flesh. By all means, try some if you find them.

An off-dry Gewürztraminer goes well with the sweetness of the persimmons in this salad.

½ cup/55 g coarsely chopped raw almonds

2 Fuyu persimmons

¼ cup/60 ml extra-virgin olive oil

1 tbsp white wine vinegar

1 tbsp balsamic vinegar

½ tsp salt

¼ tsp freshly ground pepper

3 cups/85 g arugula/rocket

Preheat the oven to 350°F/180°C/gas 4. Spread the almonds on a rimmed baking sheet/tray and toast until fragrant, 5 to 7 minutes. Remove from the oven and let cool.

Cut the top off the persimmons and peel the skin. Thinly slice the persimmons crosswise, so the starburst shows.

In a small bowl, whisk the oil with the vinegars, salt, and pepper. In a large salad bowl, toss the arugula/rocket and almonds with the vinaigrette to coat. Divide among salad plates and top each salad with slices of persimmon.

Grill-Roasted Herbed Turkey with Chardonnay Gravy

SERVES 8, WITH LEFTOVERS

Cooking a turkey on the grill in a roasting pan saves oven space for other dishes, and gets the cooks outside in the crisp fall air to check on the turkey every half hour or so. Bake the dressing in a separate casserole, and stuff the turkey cavity with aromatic herbs, onions, and lemon.

Smaller turkeys are more flavorful, and easier to cook and serve for a crowd than one gigantic bird. Look for free-range organic or heritage birds for even better flavor.

An aromatic white wine, like a spicy Gewürztraminer, is lovely with turkey. For red wine fans, a juicy Zinfandel is a good choice.

1 cup/225 g unsalted butter

1 bottle/750 ml Chardonnay

One turkey, 12 to 15 lb/5.5 to 6.8 kg

¼ cup/60 ml extra-virgin olive oil

2 tbsp salt

1 tbsp freshly ground pepper

1 tbsp finely chopped fresh thyme, plus sprigs for stuffing

1 tbsp finely chopped fresh sage, plus sprigs for stuffing

2 small onions, halved

1 lemon, halved

Chardonnay Gravy (recipe follows) for serving

Preheat a gas grill/barbecue to medium-high, or prepare a medium-hot fire in a charcoal grill/barbecue. In a medium saucepan, melt the butter with the Chardonnay over medium heat until simmering. Remove from heat and soak a large cheesecloth/muslin in the butter mixture.

Remove the turkey giblets from the turkey and reserve to make stock for the gravy. Rinse the turkey inside and out; dry well. In a small bowl, make a paste with the olive oil, salt, pepper, and finely chopped herbs. Rub the outside of the turkey with the herb paste and place it on a rack in a roasting pan/tray, breast side up. Tuck the wing tips under the turkey. Stuff the body cavity with the onion and lemon halves and the herb sprigs.

Drape the soaked cheesecloth/muslin over the breast of the turkey, covering the top portion of the leg as well. Reserve the remaining Chardonnay butter for basting.

Place the roasting pan/tray on the grill/barbecue and close the cover. Roast for 30 minutes, then uncover the grill/barbecue and baste the cheesecloth/muslin with the Chardonnay butter mixture, using a pastry brush. If the bottom of the roasting pan/tray is dry, add ½ cup/120 ml water to keep the drippings from burning. Reduce heat to medium, cover, and roast, basting the cheesecloth/muslin every 30 minutes, for another hour and a half. Add a little more water if the bottom of the pan is dry.

continued

FALL: TRADITIONAL WINE COUNTRY THANKSGIVING **161**

Discard the cheesecloth/muslin and baste the turkey with the pan juices. Cover again and roast for another 45 minutes to 1 hour, for a total of 2¾ to 3 hours, or until an instant-read thermometer inserted in the thigh but not touching bone registers 165°F/74°C (the turkey will continue to cook as it rests.) Transfer the turkey to a carving board, tent with aluminum foil, and let rest for at least 20 minutes. Pour the drippings through a fine-mesh sieve into a 4-cup/960-ml glass measure, then skim off the fat and reserve. Reserve the roasting pan/tray for making the gravy. Carve the turkey and serve with Chardonnay Gravy.

Chardonnay Gravy ‖ MAKES 3 CUPS

Reserved giblets, roasting pan/tray, drippings, and fat from Grill-Roasted Herbed Turkey (preceding recipe)

6 cups/1.4 l water

2 celery stalks, chopped

1 onion, coarsely chopped, plus 1½ cups/215 g finely chopped onions

1 carrot, peeled and chopped

1 cup/240 ml Chardonnay wine

4 tbsp/55 g unsalted butter

¼ cup/30 g Wondra flour

Salt and freshly ground pepper

In a medium saucepan, combine the giblets, water, celery, the coarsely chopped onion, and the carrot. Bring to a boil over medium-high heat, then reduce to a simmer and cook for 2 hours or so, skimming the surface occasionally. Remove from heat and strain. You should have 2 cups/480 ml turkey stock. Use now, or cover and refrigerate.

In a medium saucepan, bring the turkey stock to a low simmer. Place the roasting pan/tray over two burners on the stove top. Over medium-high heat, add the Chardonnay and turkey stock to the pan and stir to scrape up the browned bits from the bottom of the pan. Cook to reduce the liquid by half. Pour through a fine-mesh sieve into a glass measure or pitcher.

In the roasting pan/tray, melt the butter with the reserved turkey fat over medium heat and cook the finely chopped onions for 15 minutes, stirring occasionally, until lightly browned. Sprinkle the flour into the pan and whisk in salt and pepper to taste. Cook, whisking constantly, for 2 minutes. Add the hot stock and cook, whisking occasionally, for 5 minutes, or until thickened.

Winter Squash Gratin with Caramelized Onions, Chiles, and Thyme || SERVES 8

Our farmer neighbor, Montana, sent over a big wooden box of winter squash, onions, and chiles, and this gratin was born out of that cornucopia. I sent him some wine in return, and we both were happy! You can use acorn or butternut squash here, but Delicata, Hubbard, and Kabocha squash are fun alternatives. The heat of the chiles contrasts with the sweetness of the squash and caramelized onions.

2 tbsp extra-virgin olive oil

2 red onions, finely sliced

2 jalapeño chiles, finely chopped

3 lb/1.4 kg winter squash, such as Delicata, acorn, or butternut

1 tsp salt

½ tsp freshly ground pepper

2 tsp finely chopped fresh thyme

1 cup/240 ml heavy/double cream

Preheat the oven to 350°F/180°C/gas 4. In a large sauté pan, heat the olive oil over medium heat until shimmering. Add the onions and sauté until lightly browned, about 10 minutes. Add the chiles and sauté for 5 minutes. Remove from heat and let cool.

Cut the squash in half lengthwise and scoop out the seeds. Cut off the skin. Place the squash, cut side down, on a cutting board and cut into ¼-in/6-mm slices.

In a gratin dish, overlap half of the squash slices. Sprinkle with ½ tsp of the salt, ¼ tsp of the pepper, and half of the thyme. Evenly spread the caramelized onions on top. Repeat with the remaining squash, then the remaining ½ tsp salt and ¼ tsp pepper. Sprinkle with the remaining thyme. Pour the cream over and cover with aluminum foil. Bake for 30 minutes and then remove the foil and bake for another 30 minutes, or until the squash is tender and the cream is absorbed.

Preheat the broiler/grill. Place the gratin under the broiler/grill, 5 in/12 cm from the heat source, for 3 to 5 minutes, or until lightly browned.

Brussels Sprouts Braised in White Wine with Pancetta || SERVES 8

This dish couldn't be easier, and it tastes even better the next day. In my opinion, everything tastes better with a little wine and bacon, and Brussels sprouts are no exception. Pancetta, which is unsmoked Italian bacon, gives this dish a satisfyingly savory flavor. One of my favorite Sonoma County restaurateurs, John Stewart, makes his own pancetta, and that's what I use, but you can readily find pancetta at the market now. You can also substitute prosciutto, which is not smoked but is quite a bit leaner than pancetta, and its flavor more subtle.

2 lb/910 g Brussels sprouts, halved lengthwise

4 oz/115 g pancetta, cut into small dice

½ cup/120 ml dry white wine, such as Chardonnay

Salt and freshly ground pepper

In a large pot of salted boiling water, cook the Brussels sprouts until crisp-tender, about 5 minutes. Drain. In a large sauté pan, sauté the pancetta over medium heat until the pancetta is browned and the fat is rendered, about 5 minutes. Stir in the wine and cook to reduce by half. Add the Brussels sprouts and toss to combine. Season with salt and pepper.

Baby Turnips Braised in Sweet Butter | SERVES 8

The first baby turnips of the season are sweet and have a wonderful, firm texture; they're a far cry from the big, starchy turnips you see in midwinter. This easy recipe uses one of my favorite methods for cooking vegetables: rather than blanching the vegetables and then sautéing, I braise them in their own juices right in the sauté pan. It saves a couple of steps and results in delicious crisp-tender vegetables. (Reserve the turnip greens to sauté another night.)

1½ lb/680 g baby turnips, about 2 in/5 cm in diameter

2 tbsp unsalted butter

1 tbsp extra-virgin olive oil

1 tsp salt

½ tsp freshly ground pepper

Trim the turnips and reserve the greens for another use, leaving ¼ in/6 mm of stem on each turnip. Peel and halve the turnips.

In a medium sauté pan, melt the butter with the olive oil over medium heat until foaming. Add the turnips and toss to coat. Reduce heat to low, cover, and cook for about 5 minutes, or until tender. Add the salt and pepper; taste and adjust the seasoning.

Gravenstein Apple and Dried Cranberry Tart ‖ SERVES 8

I love these free-form tarts for entertaining, and for Thanksgiving, you've got plenty of other prep to do without having to worry about a perfectly formed pie crust. You don't have to blind bake the tart shell, so the tart cooks in an hour while you're prepping the rest of your meal.

I use Gravenstein apples in this recipe, grown locally in the nearby town of Sebastopol, but any tart apple will do. The wine-soaked dried cranberries here make it really feel like Thanksgiving. I like to poach dried fruit in our own late-harvest Sauvignon Blanc, but any dessert wine or even port would serve you well. Serve the tart with whichever dessert wine you've chosen to make the tart.

PASTRY DOUGH

1¼ cup/130 g all-purpose/plain flour

⅛ tsp salt

2 tsp sugar

7 tbsp/100 g cold unsalted butter, cut into chunks

3 tbsp ice water

FILLING

2 tbsp sugar

4 to 5 Gravenstein or other tart apples, peeled, cored, and cut into slices ½ inch/12 mm thick

½ cup/115 g dried cranberries

1 cup/240 ml dessert wine, such as late-harvest Sauvignon Blanc, Sauternes, or port

1 large egg, beaten

Vanilla Ice Cream (page 112) for serving

For the dough: In a food processor, pulse together the flour, salt, and sugar. Add the butter and pulse until the mixture resembles pebbles. Add the ice water, 1 tbsp at a time, and pulse just until the mixture comes together. Do not form into a ball. Turn out onto a floured surface and shape into a disk. Wrap in plastic wrap and refrigerate for at least 30 minutes or up to 2 days.

Adjust an oven rack in the center of the oven. Preheat the oven to 375°F/190°C/gas 5.

For the filling: In a large bowl, stir together the sugar and apples. In a small saucepan, combine the cranberries and wine. Bring to a simmer over medium-low heat and cook until the cranberries are plump, about 10 minutes. Remove from heat and let cool slightly. Drain, reserving the liquid. Add the cranberries to the apple mixture, along with 2 tbsp of the reserved liquid. Toss to combine.

Remove the tart dough from the refrigerator and let soften for a few minutes. Roll out on a piece of parchment/baking paper to about 12 in/30.5 cm in diameter. Transfer the paper and dough to a baking sheet/tray. Pile the fruit mixture in the center of the dough and fold the dough up around the fruit, pinching to make a seam every 2 in/5 cm. There should be at least 6 in/15 cm of fruit showing. Brush the pastry edges liberally with the beaten egg.

Bake for 45 to 50 minutes, or until the crust is golden brown and the apples are tender. Remove from the oven and transfer the tart to a wire rack/cake cooler. Serve warm or at room temperature, with ice cream.

Why do restaurants charge a fee when you bring your own wine?

This fee is called corkage, and most restaurants do it to make up for the profit lost from you not purchasing a bottle from their list. Wine is a significant profit center for restaurants, which have very narrow profit margins to begin with. Restaurants usually mark up their wines 2½ to 3 times for their lists. Some restaurants will waive corkage if you also buy a bottle, which is good etiquette as a diner. Restaurants generally take great care in putting together their wine lists and deserve appreciation for them. By all means, don't bring a bottle of wine that's already on their list. And if you bring a very expensive bottle, do ask the sommelier if he or she would like to taste it, also good dining etiquette. If you're still irritated at the thought of paying corkage, remember that the restaurant still has to open and serve your wine and wash the wineglasses at the end of the night.

Mediterranean-Style Thanksgiving

○ ○ ○

Grilled Radicchio Salad with Gorgonzola and Balsamic Vinaigrette / 171

Winter Squash and Sage Risotto / 172

Broccoli Rabe with White Wine and Red Pepper / 173

Pork Roast Stuffed with Kalamata Olives and Oregano / 175

Honey-Walnut Semolina Cake with Dried Figs and Bittersweet Chocolate / 176

Here in Sonoma wine country, we have lots of Italian wine families, so when I think of Thanksgiving, I think of a Mediterranean version of a late-fall feast. Pinot Grigio is a natural choice for a white wine here, and a Cal-Ital Sangiovese is perfect with the pork roast.

Grilled Radicchio Salad with Gorgonzola and Balsamic Vinaigrette ‖ SERVES 6

In winemaking, we watch for bitterness as the wines develop, and take steps to remove it if necessary, so I'm naturally sensitive to bitterness on the palate. Grilling radicchio turns it from bitter to smoky, tender, and slightly sweet. The sweetness of the balsamic and the pungency of the Gorgonzola add complexity to this Mediterranean salad.

Pinot Grigio's zingy acidity is a nice foil for the richness of the Gorgonzola in the salad.

3 small heads radicchio, quartered

¼ cup/60 ml extra-virgin olive oil, plus more for brushing

1 tbsp red wine vinegar

1 tbsp balsamic vinegar

1 tsp Dijon mustard

½ tsp salt

¼ tsp freshly ground pepper

4 oz/115 g Gorgonzola cheese

Preheat a gas grill/barbecue to medium-high, or prepare a medium-hot fire in a charcoal grill/barbecue.

Brush the radicchio with olive oil. Place the radicchio on the grill/barbecue, cover, and cook for 2 to 3 minutes per side, or until grill-marked but still crunchy in the middle. Transfer to a plate.

In a small bowl, whisk together the ¼ cup/60 ml olive oil, the vinegars, Dijon, salt, and pepper. Divide the grilled radicchio among 6 salad plates and crumble the Gorgonzola on top. Drizzle with the vinaigrette and serve.

Winter Squash and Sage Risotto || SERVES 6

Is anything more comforting than risotto? It's creamy, savory, and totally satisfying. When I make it for a crowd, I usually perch my guests at the island looking into the kitchen, so I can chat and stir at the same time. In fall, I love the combination of aromatic sage and winter squash. The firm texture of butternut squash allows it to keep its shape during all that stirring, and its sweetness complements the savory broth and the Parmesan.

The rich risotto stands up to the acidity in a medium-bodied Sangiovese, but a Pinot Grigio will also perform well here, even after the salad course.

6 cups/1.4 l chicken stock

2 tbsp extra-virgin olive oil

2 tbsp finely chopped fresh sage

1 onion, finely chopped

1 lb/455 g butternut squash, peeled, seeded, and cut into ½-in/12-mm dice (about 3 cups/340 g)

2 cups/430 g Arborio rice

1 cup/240 ml dry white wine

2 tbsp unsalted butter

⅓ cup/40 g grated Parmesan cheese

In a large saucepan, bring the stock to a simmer and maintain it over low heat.

In a heavy, large saucepan, heat the olive oil over medium-high heat until shimmering. Add the sage and sauté until fragrant. Add the onion and sauté until translucent, about 5 minutes. Add the squash and sauté for several minutes more. Add the rice and toss to coat. Add half of the wine and stir until the liquid is absorbed. Add the stock, one ladleful at a time, stirring after each addition until the liquid is absorbed. Add the remaining wine and stir until the rice is al dente, a total of about 20 minutes. Stir in the butter and Parmesan and serve.

Broccoli Rabe with White Wine and Red Pepper || SERVES 6

Broccoli rabe grows like a champ in my garden in late fall and early winter. Its slightly bitter and spicy bite works beautifully with a bit of heat from red pepper flakes. Braising vegetables in white wine rather than water adds a punch of flavor.

1 tbsp extra-virgin olive oil

2 garlic cloves, sliced thinly

½ tsp red pepper flakes

2 bunches broccoli rabe, chopped

¼ cup/60 ml dry white wine, such as Pinot Grigio

1 tsp salt

½ tsp freshly ground pepper

In a large sauté pan, heat the olive oil over medium heat until shimmering. Add the garlic and sauté for 1 minute; do not brown. Add the red pepper flakes and stir to combine.

Add the broccoli rabe, white wine, salt, and pepper. Cover and cook for 5 to 7 minutes, or until the broccoli rabe is crisp-tender.

Pork Roast Stuffed with Kalamata Olives and Oregano || SERVES 6 TO 8

This recipe was born as a result of staring at a gorgeous pork loin and the contents of my refrigerator! Make your life easy and get pitted kalamatas. Fresh oregano makes the pork sing a Mediterranean song. Roasted fennel is bathed in the pork juices and caramelizes just beautifully. A juicy Sangiovese is just right for this Italian-inspired dish.

½ cup/85 g chopped kalamata olives

3 garlic cloves, finely chopped

¼ cup/10 g finely chopped fresh oregano

1 tbsp Dijon mustard

2 tbsp plus 1 tsp extra-virgin olive oil

One 3-lb/1.4-kg boneless pork loin

1 tbsp salt, plus 1 tsp

2 tsp freshly ground pepper, plus ¼ tsp

3 fennel bulbs, trimmed and quartered lengthwise

½ cup/120 ml Pinot Noir or other dry red wine

½ cup/120 ml beef stock

Preheat the oven to 400°F/200°C/gas 6. In a small bowl, combine the olives, garlic, oregano, mustard, and the 2 tbsp olive oil and stir to blend. Set aside.

Season the pork loin on all sides with 1 tbsp salt and 2 tsp pepper. Cut the pork loin in half horizontally about two-thirds of the way through. Spread the olive stuffing inside the pork loin and tie it closed in three places with kitchen twine. In a small bowl, toss the fennel in the 1 tsp olive oil, and the remaining salt and pepper.

Place the pork loin on a rack in a roasting pan/tray, scattering the fennel in the bottom of the pan. Roast for 30 minutes, then check the fennel to see if it's tender.

If so, transfer to a plate and keep warm. Roast the pork for another 10 minutes, or until a meat thermometer inserted into the thickest part of the pork loin registers 145°F/63°C. Transfer the roast to a carving board and tent with aluminum foil; let rest for at least 10 minutes.

Place the roasting pan/tray over two burners on the stove top and turn the heat to medium-high. Add the wine to the pan and stir to scrape up the browned bits on the bottom of the pan. Add the stock and cook to reduce by half. Strain through a fine-mesh sieve, reserving the jus.

Cut the pork into thin slices and serve, accompanied with the fennel and drizzled with the jus.

Honey-Walnut Semolina Cake with Dried Figs and Bittersweet Chocolate ‖ SERVES 8

This is my riff on a traditional Eastern Mediterranean sweet, similar to baklava but made with semolina flour rather than phyllo. Italians use semolina flour as well, both in sweets and, of course, in pasta dough. It gives this cake a more rustic crumb. The addition of figs is typical of the Mediterranean. Bittersweet chocolate isn't indigenous to the Middle East, but I've added it with a nod to Sicilian desserts that incorporate chocolate into the more typical combination of honey, nuts, and dried fruit. Our bees' handiwork makes an appearance here, but any kind of honey will do. I serve the cake with cardamom ice cream, simply made by steeping cardamom pods in the milk of the custard base.

1½ cups/170 g walnut pieces

1 cup/130 g semolina flour

1½ tsp baking powder

½ tsp salt

¾ cup/170 g unsalted butter at room temperature

½ cup/120 ml honey

¼ cup/50 g sugar

½ tsp vanilla extract/essence

3 large eggs

⅓ cup/50 g chopped dried Mission figs

12 oz/340 g bittersweet chocolate chopped

Cardamom Ice Cream (facing page) for serving

Adjust an oven rack in the center of the oven. Preheat the oven to 350°F/180°C/gas 4. Butter and flour a 9-in/23-cm cake pan/tin; knock out the excess flour.

Spread the walnuts on a rimmed baking sheet/tray and toast in the oven for about 5 minutes, or until fragrant. Pour into a bowl and let cool.

In a food processor, combine the toasted walnuts and semolina flour; grind until very fine. Add the baking powder and salt and pulse to combine. Set aside.

In a stand mixer fitted with the paddle attachment, cream the butter, honey, and sugar until light and fluffy, about 3 minutes. Scrape down the sides of the bowl. Add the

vanilla and mix to incorporate. Add the eggs, one at a time, beating well after each addition and stopping to scrape down the sides of the bowl. Beat in the nut mixture until blended. Stir in the figs and chocolate until just incorporated.

Spread the batter evenly in the prepared pan/tin. Bake for 35 to 40 minutes, or until a toothpick inserted in the center of the cake comes out clean.

Transfer the cake to a wire rack/cake cooler and let cool completely. Run a knife around the edge of the pan and unmold the cake onto a plate. Cut into wedges and serve with cardamom ice cream.

Cardamom Ice Cream || MAKES 1½ QT/1.4 L

2½ cups/600 ml heavy/double cream
2 cups/480 ml whole milk
8 whole cardamom pods

2 teaspoons ground cardamom
8 large egg yolks

1 cup sugar
¼ tsp salt

In a medium saucepan, combine the cream, milk, and cardamom pods. Cook over low heat for 5 minutes, or until bubbles form around the edges of the pan. Do not simmer. Remove from heat, whisk in the ground cardamom, cover, and let stand for 30 minutes.

Remove the cardamom pods. Using an electric mixer, beat the egg yolks, sugar, and salt on high speed until the mixture has doubled in volume. Reduce the speed to medium. Gradually beat in 1 cup/240 ml of the cream mixture to temper. Again add 1 cup/240 ml of the mixture and beat to combine. Return to the saucepan and cook over low heat, stirring often, until the mixture is thick enough to coat the back of a spoon, about 5 minutes. Remove from heat and strain into a medium bowl set in an ice bath. Let cool completely. Cover and refrigerate for at least 2 hours or overnight.

Freeze in an ice cream maker according to the manufacturer's instructions.

Winter

Most people love to entertain in summer. They find summer menus of grilled meats and colorful salads easy to do and comfortingly casual. Don't get me wrong. I love to entertain in the summer, too, but winter entertaining can be equally easy. There is something so cozy about being welcomed in from the outdoor chill to a living room with a roaring fireplace. Instead of spending Saturday in the garden, the cook has more time to be inside the kitchen, making prep a little less frantic. And no worries about heating up the kitchen on a hot summer day. Instead, we love the warmth the oven gives off while the scent of homemade dessert fills the house. Many of my favorite winter dishes are long, slow braises that can be made hours ahead of my guests' arrival, or even the day before.

While summertime entertaining is super casual, I love the shift to more elegant winter entertaining. Out come finer linen napkins, my good silver, wineglasses I'm not worried will crash to the patio floor. Instead of serving my guests in shorts and a T-shirt, I dress up a little, although in wine country that might only mean a cashmere sweater and pair of heels to go with tried-and-true jeans. Longer discussions ensue around the table as the tapers melt down, and red-wine glasses are filled and refilled. Coffee and tea is offered, and guests linger, not anxious to leave the cocoon of your home for the chilly night outside. It's wonderful to entertain in winter. Here are several menus to show you how to do it in wine country style.

The Winter Garden

Hardy vegetables are prolific in the winter garden, with emerald green kale, tight heads of brilliant white cauliflower, deep red chard, and mustard greens standing in the naturally moist soil. Requiring so little care, the winter garden reminds us that there is still an outside world even when we spend most of our time indoors. It's easy to forget about the garden when night falls at 5 P.M., but a stroll out into the winter garden on a sun-warmed Saturday afternoon similarly warms the soul. It's lovely to cut sturdy greens for braising, while root vegetables and winter squash round out the winter menu. Mason jars filled with dried legumes inspire soups and stews, perfect on cold winter days. Hearty herbs like rosemary and thyme continue to grow, despite the cold, making for aromatic roasted meats and potatoes. And citrus fruits lift the spirits in wintertime, offering inspiration for lemon tarts and marmalades, or just a perfectly sweet tart grapefruit on a cloudy winter morning.

ASK THE WINEMAKER

I've noticed that the alcohol levels in wines seem to be getting higher. What gives?

You're right. Especially in California, with its plentiful sunshine, winemakers have been letting their grapes get nice and ripe, much riper than even a decade ago. The reason? Super-ripe grapes produce wines with intense, jammy flavors that many influential critics and consumers love. The sugar in the grapes converts to alcohol, so it makes sense that the higher the sugar levels, the higher the alcohol levels. A decade ago, wine with an alcohol content of more than 14 percent was rare, but no more.

Now, many California wines have an alcohol content of 15 percent, with some Zins edging into the 16 percent range. The downside is that these wines are so overpowering they can be difficult to pair with food. While the pendulum has swung far in the high-alcohol direction, I'm seeing some winemakers begin to move closer to the middle, looking to make intense wines that also work with food and allow you to enjoy more than one glass!

Ocean-Harvest Dinner

∘ ∘ ∘

Smoked Salmon, Cucumber, and Crème Fraîche Crostini / 185

Cracked Crab with Meyer Lemon Aioli / 186

Drunken Sonoma Cioppino / 189

Escarole Salad with Grapefruit and Avocado / 191

Gingerbread and Pear Cake with Crystallized Ginger Glaze / 192

December is the beginning of crab season. We throw newspapers on top of the kitchen island, break out our crab tools, and extract as much of that sweet crabmeat as we can. This menu takes advantage of the gorgeous winter harvest of the sea. It's all about minerally wines here, so a crisp Pinot Blanc would be terrific with the smoked salmon and the cracked crab. Go for a spicy Zin with the cioppino.

Smoked Salmon, Cucumber, and Crème Fraîche Crostini | SERVES 6 TO 8

My friend Hunt Conrad makes the most fantastic smoked salmon from fish he catches in Bodega Bay. Look for wild salmon from Oregon, Washington, and Alaska. This hors d'oeuvre couldn't be easier; it's really just a matter of assembly. The salty smoked salmon plays off the freshness of the cucumber, the creaminess of the crème fraîche, and the crunch of the crostini.

Serve a Pinot Blanc to contrast with the richness of the salmon.

18 thin slices baguette

¼ cup/60 ml extra-virgin olive oil

4 oz/115 g smoked salmon, finely chopped

1 shallot, finely chopped

2 tbsp finely chopped fresh chives

1 tsp fresh lemon juice

½ tsp freshly ground pepper

½ cup/120 ml crème fraîche

18 very thin slices English/hothouse cucumber

Lemon zest curls for garnish (made with a zest stripper)

Preheat the oven to 350°F/180°C/gas 4. Arrange the baguette slices in a single layer on a baking sheet/tray and brush lightly on the top with the olive oil. Bake until crisp on the edges but still soft in the center, about 10 minutes. Remove from the oven and transfer to wire racks/cake coolers to cool.

In a small bowl, combine the salmon, shallot, chives, lemon juice, and pepper and stir to blend. Spread crème fraîche on each toast, then top with a slice of cucumber and a mound of the smoked salmon mixture. Garnish with a curl of lemon zest.

Cracked Crab
with Meyer Lemon Aioli ‖ SERVES 6

In Northern California, crab comes into season around the beginning of December and lasts through January. It's always cause for celebration, and feels so holiday festive. Buy the freshest cooked whole crabs you can find, and have your fishmonger prepare them for eating.

A simple lemon-spiked aioli is all the adornment fresh crab needs. The sweetness of Meyer lemons is a nice foil for the briny crabmeat.

Invite some close friends over, throw newspapers on the table, and go to town with crab crackers, lots of napkins, and crisp white Pinot Blanc.

LEMON AIOLI

3 garlic cloves, finely chopped

2 large egg yolks

1 tsp grated Meyer lemon zest

Juice of 1 Meyer lemon

1 tsp salt

½ tsp freshly ground pepper

1 cup/240 ml extra-virgin olive oil

3 cooked Dungeness crabs, cleaned, legs removed and cracked

For the aioli: In a food processor, combine the garlic, egg yolks, lemon zest, juice, salt, and pepper. Pulse to combine. With the machine running, gradually add the olive oil in a slow stream until emulsified. Taste and adjust the seasoning.

Serve the crab on a large platter with a bowl of aioli for people to help themselves. Provide another bowl for crab shells, and lemon water and towels for cleaning hands.

Drunken Sonoma Cioppino || SERVES 6

Cioppino hails from San Francisco, but my version showcases seafood harvested in Sonoma's Bodega Bay. I call it "drunken" because the soup base is made with lots of red wine! Use whatever seafood is the absolute freshest you can find. I've omitted crab here, since we started the menu with cracked crab, but feel free to add.

Cioppino, a great communal dish, demands a loosening of table manners as you toss spent clam and mussel shells, and sop up the juices with crusty bread.

This is a perfect example of food and wine rules being mutable. Red wine is the ticket with this rich cioppino, because of the red wine and tomatoes in the stew. A spicy Zinfandel from Paso Robles or Sonoma's Dry Creek Valley would be just perfect.

2 tbsp extra-virgin olive oil

1 large onion, finely chopped

4 garlic cloves

2 anchovies, mashed

1 bay leaf

1 tbsp finely chopped fresh oregano

½ fennel bulb, trimmed, cored, and finely diced (fronds reserved)

1 red bell pepper/capsicum, seeded, deveined, and finely diced

1 jalapeño chile, seeded and finely chopped

2 tbsp tomato paste/tomato puree

2 cups/480 ml dry red wine

2 cups/480 ml good-quality fish stock

One 28-oz/800-g can whole tomatoes with juice

18 clams, scrubbed

18 mussels, scrubbed, and debearded if needed

1 lb/455 g red snapper, cut into 2-in/5-cm pieces

1 lb/455 g tiger shrimp/prawns

1 lb/455 g sea scallops, halved if large

2 tbsp finely chopped fresh flat-leaf parsley for garnish

In a large, heavy soup pot, heat the olive oil over medium heat until shimmering. Add the onion and sauté until translucent, about 3 minutes. Add the garlic, anchovies, bay leaf, and oregano and sauté for 2 minutes. Add the fennel, bell pepper/capsicum, and jalapeño and sauté for 2 to 3 minutes more, until slightly softened. Stir in the tomato paste/tomato puree, then the red wine, fish stock, and tomatoes, breaking the tomatoes up with the back of a wooden spoon. Adjust heat to a simmer, cover, and cook for 30 minutes. Taste and adjust the seasoning. The stew base can be made a day ahead, before adding the seafood.

Add the clams and mussels to the simmering stew base, cover, and cook until the shellfish have opened, 3 to 5 minutes. Using a slotted spoon, transfer the clams and mussels to a bowl. Discard any shellfish that haven't opened. Add the red snapper, shrimp/prawns, and scallops to the pot and cook for 3 minutes, or until the shrimp/prawns are evenly pink. Return the clams and mussels to the pot and heat for 1 minute. Serve in shallow soup bowls, garnished with the parsley and reserved finely diced fennel fronds.

Escarole Salad
with Grapefruit and Avocado || SERVES 6

Grapefruit brightens up everything with its sweet and tangy punch, a perfect complement to velvety avocado and slightly bitter winter salad greens. Avocados are more abundant in Southern California than in the northern part of the state, but some are produced slightly inland from the coast. The Hass variety has a dark, thick, and bumpy skin, and makes up 95 percent of the avocado crop in California. I find them easier to peel, and their texture more creamy than that of other varieties.

¼ cup/60 ml extra-virgin olive oil

1 tbsp Champagne vinegar

1 tsp balsamic vinegar

½ tsp salt

¼ tsp freshly ground pepper

Leaves from 1 head escarole/
Batavian endive, torn

1 large ruby grapefruit, skin and pith cut off, cut between membranes into segments

1 large Hass avocado, peeled, pitted, and cut into 1-in/2.5-cm chunks

In a small bowl, whisk together the oil, vinegars, salt, and pepper.

In a large salad bowl, toss the escarole/Batavian endive with the vinaigrette and let stand for several minutes to wilt slightly. Add the grapefruit sections and avocado and toss gently to combine. Divide among 6 plates and serve.

Gingerbread and Pear Cake
with Crystallized Ginger Glaze ‖ SERVES 8 TO 10

Pears from the Dry Creek Valley of Sonoma take center stage in this dessert. In fact, before grapes became the major crop here, pears and prunes dominated our fields, so this cake feels like an homage to our Sonoma County heritage. But any kind of ripe pear will work in this moist cake.

While baking, this cake makes the whole house smell divine. The crystallized ginger in the glaze is a wonderful surprise.

1½ cups/195 g all-purpose/plain flour

1 tsp baking soda/bicarbonate of soda

½ tsp salt

1 tsp ground ginger

½ tsp ground cloves

½ tsp ground cinnamon

¼ tsp ground allspice

½ cup/120 ml molasses/treacle

¼ cup/60 ml hot water

½ cup/115 g unsalted butter, melted

½ cup/100 g packed brown sugar/
    Demerara sugar

3 large eggs

1 ripe pear, peeled, cored, and cut
    into 1-in/2.5 cm chunks

CRYSTALLIZED GINGER GLAZE

2 tbsp crystallized ginger

½ cup/50 g confectioners'/icing sugar

¼ cup/60 ml water

Vanilla-flavored whipped cream
    for serving

Adjust an oven rack in the center of the oven. Preheat the oven to 350°F/180°C/gas 4. Butter and flour a 9-in/23-cm springform cake pan/tin, knocking out the excess flour.

Sift together the flour, baking soda/bicarbonate of soda, salt, ginger, cloves, cinnamon, and allspice into a medium bowl and set aside.

In a stand mixer, beat the molasses/treacle and hot water together until combined. Add the butter and brown sugar/Demerara sugar and beat until combined. Add the eggs, one at a time, beating well. Add half of the flour mixture to the batter and beat until just incorporated. Add the remaining flour mixture and beat until just combined, stopping to scrape down the sides of the bowl.

Pour the batter into the prepared pan. Scatter the top of the batter evenly with the pear pieces. Bake until a cake tester inserted in the center of the cake comes out clean, about 40 minutes. Transfer to a wire rack/cake cooler and let cool for 10 minutes.

Meanwhile, for the glaze: If the crystallized ginger pieces are very large and hard, pulse them in a mini food processor to make the pieces smaller, or chop them by hand with a large knife. In a small saucepan, combine the ginger with the confectioners'/icing sugar and water over medium heat. Swirl to combine and cook until bubbling, 2 or 3 minutes total. Remove from heat.

Unmold the cake onto a wire rack/cake cooler set on a baking sheet/tray. Using a wooden or metal skewer, poke holes all the way through the cake. Drizzle the glaze uniformly over the top of the cake. Serve warm or at room temperature, with whipped cream.

Winter Dinner Party

○ ○ ○

Prosciutto-Roasted Fennel / 195

Cream of Chanterelle Soup / 196

Syrah-Braised Lamb Shanks with Garlicky White Beans / 197

Chocolate Bread Pudding with Port / 200

In winter, I start a braise in the afternoon and take my time setting the dining room table with candles, flowers, and my good silver. As night falls, we light a big fire in the fireplace, pull several bottles of red wine out of the cellar, and a good time is had by all.

Lamb shanks are a perfect make-ahead dish, and they're even better when cooked a day or two before serving. Prosciutto-wrapped fennel is an easy appetizer to accompany the first glass of wine. Opt for an aromatic and lush Viognier to start, and move to a rustic Syrah to pair with the lamb.

Prosciutto-Roasted Fennel || SERVES 6 TO 8

I have a whole prosciutto ham hanging in my basement. Really. It hangs just above a case or two of Pinot Noir. I figure what grows together goes together. After we successfully bid on our neighbor's pig at the Future Farmers Fair, we had a lot of meat to use up. Huge fans of prosciutto, we thought we'd join the Italians and figure out how to make it ourselves. Not wanting to kill either ourselves or our guests, we turned to a professional chef, our friend John Stewart. John cures all manner of pork products in the Italian style, from prosciutto to coppa to pancetta, and serves them in his two restaurants, Zazu and Bovolo. He gave us lengthy instructions, and fifteen months later we had our very own prosciutto.

This recipe combines the saltiness of prosciutto with the sweetness and crunch of roasted fennel. A warm appetizer is lovely in winter, and this one takes just a few minutes to make. Serve it with olives and some bread or crostini, and your first course is complete.

Pour a lush Viognier with this dish. A little richer than Sauvignon Blanc, Viognier's rounded flavors go well with the savory prosciutto and caramelized fennel.

2 small fennel bulbs, trimmed, halved lengthwise, and cored

16 paper-thin slices prosciutto

Preheat the oven to 400°F/200°C/gas 6. Cut each fennel half into quarters. Wrap each fennel spear with a slice of prosciutto. Place on a baking sheet/tray and roast for 10 minutes, or until the prosciutto is lightly browned.

Cream of Chanterelle Soup   ‖   SERVES 6

Chanterelles appear here in winter under manzanita trees a few days after a rain. Mushroom foraging is a major pastime in Sonoma and Mendocino Counties, and chanterelles are easy to spot because of their golden color and uniquely ragged caps.

A bag of chanterelles from our tasting-room staffer's hillside property in northern Santa Rosa became the inspiration for this recipe. On a cold and rainy night, this creamy soup is a rich, satisfying way to begin a meal. Substitute other mushrooms if you can't find chanterelles. The peach overtones of Viognier complement the delicate peach aromatics of the chanterelles, but you could also pair the soup with Pinot Noir. The earthiness of the mushrooms works beautifully with earthy Pinot.

2 tbsp unsalted butter

3 small shallots, finely chopped

12 oz/340 g chanterelle mushrooms, coarsely chopped

¼ cup/60 ml Pinot Noir

3 cups/720 ml good-quality chicken stock, plus more as needed

1 tsp finely chopped fresh thyme

¼ cup/60 ml heavy/double cream

Salt and freshly ground pepper

In a heavy, medium soup pot, melt the butter over medium heat until foaming. Add the shallots and sauté until translucent, about 5 minutes. Add the mushrooms and sauté for another 5 minutes. Add the wine and stir to scrape up the browned bits from the bottom of the pan. Stir in the 3 cups/720 ml chicken stock, increase heat to medium high, and bring to a boil. Immediately reduce heat to a simmer and cook for 15 minutes.

Drain the mushroom mixture in a sieve over a bowl, reserving the liquid. Puree the mushrooms and shallots in a food processor or blender and return to the pan with the reserved liquid. Add the thyme, cream, and salt and pepper to taste. Simmer for 5 minutes, thinning with additional chicken stock if needed.

Syrah-Braised Lamb Shanks with Garlicky White Beans

SERVES 6

This is my staple winter dinner-party dish. There's something soulful and comforting about a long-braised dish like this, particularly on a cold evening. The recipe is practically foolproof, and can be made up to two days ahead. Just reheat when you're ready to serve. Make sure your butcher gives you shanks small enough to fit in your pot. One time I sent Jake to the market and he returned with enormous Flintstone-sized shanks. We actually had to cut them in half with a (clean) table saw!

A rustic, peppery Syrah would be a great complement to the lamb.

Six 4-in-/10-cm-long lamb shanks

1 tbsp salt

2 tsps black pepper

2 tbsp extra-virgin olive oil

1 large onion, chopped

2 garlic cloves, finely chopped

2 carrots, peeled and chopped

2 celery stalks, chopped

1 tsp finely chopped fresh rosemary

2 cups/480 ml Syrah or other
 dry red wine

2 cups/480 ml beef stock

Garlicky White Beans (page 198) for
 serving

Season the shanks with the salt and pepper. In a large, heavy pot, heat the olive oil over medium-high heat until shimmering. Brown the lamb shanks on all sides and transfer to a plate. Add the onion, garlic, carrots, and celery to the pot and sauté for 5 minutes. Add the rosemary and sauté for 3 minutes. Add the wine, beef stock, and browned lamb shanks to the pot. Reduce the heat to low, cover, and simmer for 2 hours, or until the meat begins to fall off the bone.

Spoon beans onto each plate and serve a lamb shank on top of each serving, along with some of the pan sauce.

Garlicky White Beans | SERVES 6

2 cups/400 g dried cannellini or
Great Northern white beans

4 garlic cloves, peeled

2 rosemary sprigs

1 tbsp salt

½ tsp freshly ground pepper

Rinse and pick over the beans. Soak overnight in water to cover by 2 in/5 cm.

Drain the beans, add to a large soup pot, and add water to cover by 2 in/5 cm. Add the garlic, rosemary, salt, and pepper and bring to a boil. Reduce heat to a simmer, cover, and cook until tender, about 45 minutes. Remove the rosemary sprigs. Taste and adjust the seasoning.

ASK THE WINEMAKER

*I went to dinner the other night at a restaurant whose wine list
was indecipherable. I gave up and ordered a cocktail instead.
How do I navigate next time?*

Some restaurants pride themselves on sourcing limited-production wines from small wineries, and Italian restaurants sometimes choose exclusively Italian wines for their lists, often from less-well-known regions. If you're a tried-and-true California wine buff, a quick scan of the list might reveal not a single familiar wine. The best tactic is to ask, though with all due respect to wait staffs, they don't always know about the wines and may point you to what's most popular, rather than what might work best for your dish and your budget. This is where the sommelier comes in.

The best tactic for communicating with a sommelier is to be crystal clear, as in "I'm looking for a red wine like a Pinot Noir, and I don't want to spend more than $60." This will spare you the agony of the sommelier fishing around to determine your price range. Giving him or her a reference point, both in wine type and in price, avoids embarrassment on both sides. Chances are good that the sommelier can point you in an interesting direction, and you will have an opportunity to try a wine you would never have known about. The wonderful thing about wine is that there's so much to learn. Take advantage of it!

Chocolate Bread Pudding with Port || SERVES 6

Our fellow vintner neighbors and frequent dinner guests, the Simpkins, are self-professed chocoholics, and this dessert wins kudos every time we serve it to them. Even the no-dessert crowd can't resist bread pudding, particularly the chocolate variety. It never disappoints on a winter night, and this one gets an added boost from a little port in the chocolate custard.

Serve small glasses of port with the dessert, just to gild the lily.

1½ cups/360 ml heavy/double cream

½ cup/100 g sugar

½ cup/120 ml whole milk

10 oz/280 g good-quality semisweet/ plain chocolate, chopped

1 large egg

1 tbsp port

4 cups/225 g 1-in/2.5-cm cubes French bread with crust

Vanilla Ice Cream (page 112) for serving

Preheat the oven to 325°F/165°C/gas 3. In a medium saucepan, bring the cream, sugar, and milk to a simmer over medium heat, whisking until the sugar dissolves. Remove from heat. Add the chocolate and whisk until melted. Let cool.

In a large bowl, whisk the egg and port together until combined. Gradually whisk in the chocolate mixture. Add the bread to the chocolate mixture and toss to coat. Transfer to a 10-cup/2-L soufflé dish. Bake until just set in the center, about 30 minutes. Serve warm, with ice cream on the side.

What kind of wineglasses should I use?

I'm asked this question all the time because there are so many options out there. The most important thing is a glass with a bowl big enough to swirl the wine to release its aroma and flavor. Stemless glasses are trendy now, and they're perfectly fine, but along with getting fingerprints on the bowl, you will warm up the wine with your hands as you drink. That's okay for Cabernet or Zinfandel, but not so good for wines that taste best at cool temperatures, like Sauvignon Blanc or Pinot Grigio. For that reason, I prefer a glass with a stem. You do not, however, need a different wineglass for every type of wine you serve. I suggest you stock your cupboard with Champagne flutes, an all-purpose white-wine glass, and an all-purpose red-wine glass. And you don't have to spend a fortune. I have broken many a glass that costs as much as a bottle of perfume. I say spend the money on the wine, not the glasses. Titanium glasses are sold at Sur la Table, and are both inexpensive and fairly indestructible. Target sells a Riedel glass for $10 a stem. If you have the budget and interest to invest in the high-end Riedel series, then by all means, go ahead. They are fantastic glasses, and really do make the wines smell and taste their best. Just know that you will break them, so build that into your budget.

A word to those who like to entertain outside in the summer. There are some terrific polycarbonate glasses on the market that are unbreakable and don't streak and cloud like the old Lucite glasses. You can chuck them right into the dishwasher with no worries. Though I always prefer to drink out of real glass, one shattered glass and the pool needs to be drained, so I make good use of these new polycarbonate glasses during the summer, and generally pour easy-drinking quaffers, like rosé or Pinot Grigio.

Weeknight Dinner

○ ○ ○

Frisée with Piave and Pine Nuts / 203

Braised Chicken Thighs with Green Olives and Pomegranate Molasses / 204

Cumin-Scented Carrots with Tangerine Zest and Chives / 207

Toasted Bulgur with Shallots and Saffron / 208

Port-Roasted Pears and Currants with Vanilla Ice Cream / 209

Praise the humble chicken thigh, full of flavor and a weeknight-dinner savior! A quick braise with white wine, tangy pomegranate molasses, and some piquant green olives yields a simple dinner packed with flavor. A Fumé Blanc would stand up to the acidity in the olives. A Cabernet Franc is light enough in tannins to work as a red.

Frisée with Piave and Pine Nuts || SERVES 6

Frisée, or curly endive, is often served in French bistros in a salad with lardons and a soft-boiled egg. Pick small, young heads of frisée, and make sure to wash them thoroughly to remove any grit. This quintessential winter green, with its slight spicy bitterness, works beautifully with cheese. Piave is a cow's milk cheese made in the Piave River Valley region of Belluno, Italy, in the northernmost part of the Veneto province. A hard cheese, its slightly sweet and nutty flavor is similar to a young Parmigiano-Reggiano. Pine nuts are added to this salad for their delicate nutty flavor.

The richness of the cheese and pine nuts is complemented nicely by a slightly oaky Fumé Blanc.

2 tbsp pine nuts

¼ cup/60 ml extra-virgin olive oil

1 tbsp Champagne vinegar

1 tsp balsamic vinegar

½ tsp salt

¼ tsp freshly ground pepper

Leaves from 2 small heads frisée, torn

2 oz/55 g Piave or Parmigiano-Reggiano cheese, shaved into curls

Preheat the oven to 350°F/180°C/gas 4. Spread the pine nuts in a pie pan and toast in the oven until golden, about 10 minutes. Pour into a bowl and let cool.

In a small bowl, whisk together the oil, vinegars, salt, and pepper. In a salad bowl, toss the frisée with the vinaigrette and pine nuts. Add the cheese shavings and toss gently. Divide among salad plates and serve.

Braised Chicken Thighs with Green Olives and Pomegranate Molasses | SERVES 6

I invented this dish one night when we had unexpected guests for dinner, and now it's in my regular repertoire. Chicken thighs get an exotic twist here with briny green olives and sweet-tart pomegranate molasses, which adds a viscous acidity to dishes and has no real substitute. If you can't find it in your market, add some lemon juice for tartness instead, along with an additional tablespoon of honey. Or reduce some pomegranate juice.

Fruit-forward and low in tannins, Cabernet Franc is a good choice when you're serving a lighter meat like chicken or pork but still want a red wine.

6 large chicken thighs, skinned

1 tsp salt, plus more for finishing

½ tsp freshly ground pepper, plus more for finishing

1 tbsp extra-virgin olive oil

1 large onion, finely chopped

2 garlic cloves, finely chopped

½ cup/120 ml dry white wine, such as Sauvignon Blanc

1 cup/240 ml chicken stock

2 tbsp pomegranate molasses

1 tbsp honey

¼ cup/35 g chopped green olives

Toasted Bulgur with Shallots and Saffron (page 208) for serving

Finely chopped fresh flat-leaf parsley for garnish and whole olives

Season the chicken thighs with the 1 tsp salt and the ½ tsp pepper. In a large sauté pan, heat the olive oil over medium-high heat just until smoking. Add the chicken thighs and sear for a few minutes on each side until golden. Using tongs, transfer to a plate.

Reduce heat to medium. Add the onion to the pan and sauté until translucent, about 3 minutes. Add the garlic and sauté for 1 minute. Add the wine and stir to scrape up the browned bits from the bottom of the pan. Stir in the stock, pomegranate molasses, and honey. Add the chicken and simmer, uncovered, for 10 minutes. Cover, add the olives, and simmer for another 10 minutes, or until the chicken is opaque throughout. Taste and adjust the seasoning.

Serve over the bulgur in shallow bowls with the pan sauce spooned over. Garnish with parsley and olives.

Cumin-Scented Carrots with Tangerine Zest and Chives || SERVES 6

This side dish reminds me of Morocco. The carrots are tossed with earthy cumin-scented olive oil, fragrant tangerine zest, and zingy and colorful chives. We grow carrots at home (when the gophers don't get to them first) and they're very sweet. Use the smallest carrots you can find, with the greens still attached. If your carrots taste starchy, add a little honey to sweeten them up.

2 lb/910 g small carrots, peeled

1 tbsp extra-virgin olive oil

1 tsp ground cumin

½ tsp grated tangerine zest

1 tbsp finely chopped fresh chives

1 tbsp unsalted butter

2 tbsp fresh tangerine or orange juice

½ tsp salt

¼ tsp freshly ground pepper

In a covered steamer over simmering water, cook the carrots until crisp-tender, about 5 minutes. Remove from heat and set aside.

In a medium sauté pan, heat the olive oil over medium heat until fragrant. Add the cumin and sauté until fragrant. Stir in the zest, then add the carrots and toss to coat. Add the chives, butter, tangerine juice, salt, and pepper. Toss again to coat.

Toasted Bulgur with Shallots and Saffron | SERVES 6

I grew up eating bulgur in traditional Middle Eastern dishes like tabbouleh and pilafs. More interesting than rice, bulgur has a nuttiness that really comes out when you toast it prior to adding liquid in the cooking process. It takes lots of liquid to make the bulgur tender, so you'll find the proportions are different than for rice.

1 tbsp extra-virgin olive oil

1 shallot, finely chopped

1 cup/68 g bulgur wheat, No. 3 (coarse) grind

3 cups/720 ml chicken stock

Pinch of saffron threads

In a medium saucepan, heat the olive oil over medium-high heat until shimmering. Add the shallot and sauté until translucent, about 3 minutes. Add the bulgur and toast, stirring, for 3 minutes, or until very lightly browned. Add the stock and saffron threads and reduce heat to low. Cover and simmer until the liquid is absorbed and the bulgur is tender, about 20 minutes.

ASK THE WINEMAKER

Why don't more wineries make half bottles?

I get this question all the time. The reality is, they're very expensive to produce. The glass, foils, and capsules all cost the same as for a full-size bottle, but wineries can't charge the same price. However, some wineries have found a niche with half bottles, so do seek them out. And with restaurants offering more and more quality wines by the glass, consumers can experiment without committing to a full bottle. A half bottle of white at the start of the meal is a nice alternative to a couple of glasses of what they're pouring behind the bar. Or if dining alone on a business trip, it's convenient to savor a half bottle of high-quality Pinot Noir or Cabernet Sauvignon throughout the meal. Besides, you never know how long a bottle has been open behind the bar, so if you're familiar with a wine that's offered in half bottle, it's a safer bet to move in that direction.

Port-Roasted Pears and Currants with Vanilla Ice Cream ‖ SERVES 6

I made this dessert on a cold Saturday evening, and even though we were all full from dinner, we managed to eat our entire portions, scraping every last bit of caramel port sauce off the plates!

This is one of the fastest and most beautiful desserts I know. The pears and currants are started on the stove and finished in the oven. Ruby port studded with the dark currants turns the pears a beautiful color. Vanilla ice cream adds the finishing touch.

Pour the same port you used to make the pears.

2 tbsp dried currants
¼ cup/60 ml ruby port
3 ripe red pears, peeled, halved
  lengthwise, and cored

3 tbsp unsalted butter
¾ cup/150 g sugar

Vanilla Ice Cream (page 112)
  for serving

Preheat the oven to 400°F/200°C/gas 6. In a small non-reactive saucepan, combine the currants and port and simmer over medium-low heat for 5 minutes to plump the currants. Remove from heat. Put the pears in a large bowl and toss with the currant mixture.

In a large ovenproof sauté pan, melt the butter over medium heat. Add the sugar and shake to combine with the melted butter. Immediately place the pears, cut side down, in the pan and drizzle with the port mixture. Cook for about 5 minutes to dissolve the sugar. The mixture will bubble up. Transfer the pan to the oven and roast for 15 minutes, or until the pears are golden and the sauce is reduced by half. Divide the pears among 6 plates. Place a scoop of ice cream alongside each serving, and drizzle both pears and ice cream with the pan sauce.

Holiday Family Dinner

o o o

Allspice-Roasted Cashews / 211

Rosemary-Crusted Standing Rib Roast with Bordeaux Gravy / 213

Herbed Popovers / 215

Roasted Parsnips with Shallots and Sage / 216

Sautéed Jerusalem Artichokes with Lacinato Kale / 217

Winter Trifle with Cranberries and Tangerines / 219

A standing rib roast with all the trimmings is my English husband's favorite holiday meal. I've updated the traditional menu, adding herbs to the popovers and serving lots of bright, crisp winter vegetables. A colorful trifle makes a dramatic ending to the meal.

Choose an elegant Bordeaux blend from Sonoma or Napa to pair with the roast. And by all means, start with sparkling wine. It's a special occasion!

Allspice-Roasted Cashews || MAKES 2 CUPS/230 G

Do you ever notice that in a bowl of mixed nuts, the cashews always go first? There's something so addictive about their sweetness. I'm always on the lookout for interesting appetizers that will work for both white- and red-wine drinkers, and I'm particularly intrigued by appetizers that don't involve crackers or bread. (Who wants guests to fill up before dinner?) You can make the nuts entirely ahead of time, and they will keep for several days. The scent of allspice heralds the holidays.

These cashews are sublime with sparkling wine.

2 cups/230 g cashews	1 tbsp ground allspice	½ tsp freshly ground pepper
2 tbsp unsalted butter, melted	1 tsp salt	

Preheat the oven to 350°F/180°C/gas 4. Spread the cashews on a rimmed baking sheet in a single layer. Toss with the butter, allspice, salt, and pepper. Roast for 10 to 15 minutes, stirring halfway through the cooking time, or until nicely browned (watch carefully, as nuts burn easily). Pour into a bowl and serve at room temperature or slightly warm.

Rosemary-Crusted Standing Rib Roast with Bordeaux Gravy ‖ SERVES 8, WITH LEFTOVERS

This Christmas-dinner extravagance elicits oohs and aahs from everyone when it comes to the table. A simple rosemary, salt, pepper, and oil paste is rubbed on the meat, which is roasted at high temperature to seal in the juices and then finished on lower heat. The drippings and roasting pan are saved to make the gravy and popovers. The meaty ribs are wonderful the next day.

Serve with a luxuriant Bordeaux blend to stand up to the meat's elegance.

1 standing beef rib roast, 7 to 8 lb/ 3.2 to 3.6 kg

2 tbsp finely chopped fresh rosemary

1 tbsp freshly cracked pepper

1½ tbsp kosher salt

1 tbsp extra-virgin olive oil

BORDEAUX GRAVY

Reserved roasting pan/tray, fat, and drippings from the roast

1 cup/240 ml Cabernet Sauvignon or Merlot, or a Bordeaux blend

2 cups/480 ml good-quality beef stock

4 tbsp/55 g unsalted butter

1½ cups/215 g chopped onions

¼ cup/30 g Wondra flour

Salt and freshly ground pepper

Herbed Popovers (page 215)

Remove the roast from the refrigerator 1 hour before cooking to allow it to come to room temperature.

Preheat the oven to 450°F/230°C/gas 8. In a small bowl, combine the rosemary, pepper, salt, and oil to make a paste. Rub the paste all over the roast, including the rib side, then place the roast, bone side down, on a rack in a roasting pan/tray.

Roast the meat for 45 minutes. Reduce the oven temperature to 375°F/190°C/gas 5 and roast for another 45 minutes, or until an instant-read thermometer inserted in the center of the meat registers 125°F/52°C for medium-rare. The meat will continue cooking as it rests.

Transfer the roast to a carving board. Tent with aluminum foil and let rest for 20 minutes before carving. Reserve the roasting pan/tray to make the gravy. Pour the

drippings through a fine-mesh sieve into a 4-cup/960-ml glass measure, then skim off the fat and reserve the fat and drippings.

For the gravy: Place the roasting pan/tray over two burners on the stove top on medium heat. Add the wine and stock; stir to scrape up the browned bits from the bottom of the pan. Pour the liquid through a fine-mesh sieve into the defatted drippings.

In a large sauté pan, melt the butter with ¼ cup/60 ml of the reserved fat. Reduce the heat to medium-low, add the onions, and sauté for 15 minutes, or until lightly browned.

Sprinkle the flour into the pan with the onions. Cook, whisking constantly, for 3 minutes. Add the drippings mixture and cook, whisking constantly, for 5 minutes, or until thickened. Season with salt and pepper.

Herbed Popovers

||

I've added fresh herbs to my mother-in-law's recipe to update it a bit. While I like rosemary for the standing rib roast (see page 213), thyme's more subtle flavor works best with the popovers. You don't need a popover pan, though your popovers will be taller if you use one. A nonstick muffin pan will do nicely. Just make sure it's truly nonstick. One year I used a brand new aluminum muffin pan and every single popover stuck to it like barnacles on a rock! Use a little fat from the drippings of your roast to impart the most flavor.

1½ cups/185 g all-purpose/plain
    flour

½ tsp salt

1½ tbsp unsalted butter, melted

1½ cups/360 ml whole milk at room
    temperature

3 large eggs at room temperature,
    beaten

1 tsp finely chopped fresh thyme

¼ cup/60 ml reserved fat from
    Rosemary-Crusted Standing
    Rib Roast (page 213)

Adjust an oven rack in the center of the oven. Preheat the oven to 425°F/220°C/gas 7. Sift the flour and salt into a large bowl. In a medium bowl, whisk together the butter, milk, eggs, and thyme. Stir the wet ingredients into the dry ingredients just until incorporated.

Add 1 tsp reserved fat to each of 12 popover or muffin cups. Heat the pan in the oven until very hot, about 5 minutes.

Fill each cup half full of batter and bake for 30 minutes, or until puffed and golden. Do not open the oven door or the popovers will fall.

Roasted Parsnips with Shallots and Sage ‖ SERVES 6 TO 8

Parsnips, wonderfully sweet root vegetables, are terribly English. Choose young, slender ones; the mature ones are so woody, they are practically inedible. They should be roasted gently to make sure they cook all the way through without browning too much.

3 lb/1.4 kg parsnips, peeled and quartered lengthwise

1 dozen shallots, peeled

2 tbsp extra-virgin olive oil

2 tsp finely chopped fresh sage

1 tsp salt

½ tsp freshly ground pepper

Preheat the oven to 350°F/180°C/gas 4. Cut the parsnips into 2-in/5-cm crosswise pieces.

On a rimmed baking sheet/tray or in a roasting pan/tray, toss the parsnips with the shallots, oil, sage, salt, and pepper. Cover with aluminum foil and roast for 20 minutes. Remove the foil and roast for another 20 minutes, or until the parsnips are tender and lightly browned, and the shallots are nicely caramelized.

Sautéed Jerusalem Artichokes with Lacinato Kale || SERVES 6 TO 8

Lacinato kale, also known as dinosaur kale, is a hearty winter favorite that grows in our garden year-round. Here, it's combined with Jerusalem artichokes, small brown tubers also known as sunchokes. Our neighbors from Tierra Vegetables sell Jerusalem artichokes at their farm stand, along with all manner of other interesting root vegetables. If you can't find Lacinato kale, substitute any other kale or winter green.

1 tbsp extra-virgin olive oil

2 garlic cloves, finely chopped

1 lb/455 g Jerusalem artichokes, peeled and cut into ½-in/12-mm rounds

2 bunches Lacinato or other kale, tough stems discarded, coarsely chopped

1 tsp salt

½ tsp freshly ground pepper

In a large soup pot, heat the olive oil over medium heat until shimmering. Add the garlic and Jerusalem artichokes and sauté for 3 minutes. Add the kale, cover, and cook, stirring once or twice, for about 5 minutes or until wilted. Add the salt and pepper and toss to combine.

Winter Trifle with Cranberries and Tangerines || SERVES 6 TO 8

Imagine my dismay when I asked my soon-to-be husband to name his favorite dessert, and he responded, "Trifle! My mother makes a great one!" Oh, boy. My only experience with trifle was a mushy mess of booze-soaked ladyfingers, packaged custard, whipped cream, and stewed out-of-season fruit. I set about to make my own version of a trifle, one that speaks to the winter season, with pumpkin bread, homemade vanilla custard, and gingered cranberries. A bit of Grand Marnier in the whipped cream gives a nod to the old-fashioned boozy trifles. You can make the pumpkin bread and cranberries days ahead, then assemble the trifle in minutes. A trifle bowl is a nice way to show off the beautiful layers, but any glass vessel will do.

This recipe makes two loaves of pumpkin bread. Use one for the trifle and freeze the other one for later.

PUMPKIN BREAD

2½ cups/320 g all-purpose/plain flour

2 tsp baking powder

1 tsp salt

1 tsp ground ginger

½ tsp ground cloves

½ tsp ground cinnamon

¾ cup/170 g unsalted butter, melted

1 cup/200 g packed brown sugar/ Demerara sugar

1 cup/200 g granulated sugar

One 14-oz/400-g can solid-pack pumpkin

3 large eggs, beaten

VANILLA CUSTARD

1½ cups/360 ml whole milk

1 vanilla bean/pod, split lengthwise

5 large egg yolks at room temperature

½ cup/100 g granulated sugar

2 tbsp sifted cornstarch/cornflour

GINGERED CRANBERRIES

3 cups/349 g fresh or frozen cranberries

1 cup/200 g granulated sugar

Grated zest of 1 tangerine

¼ cup/60 ml fresh tangerine juice

1 tbsp grated peeled fresh ginger

WHIPPED CREAM

1 cup/240 ml cold heavy/double cream

1 tsp granulated sugar

1 tsp Grand Marnier

Ground cloves for dusting

continued

For the pumpkin bread: Adjust an oven rack in the center of the oven. Preheat the oven to 375°F/190°C/gas 5. Butter and flour two 9-by-4-in/23-by-10-cm loaf pans/tins; knock out the excess flour.

Sift the flour, baking powder, salt, ginger, cloves, and cinnamon into a large bowl. In a stand mixer fitted with the paddle attachment, beat together the butter, sugars, pumpkin, and eggs. Gradually beat in the flour mixture just until combined, stopping to scrape down the sides of the bowl once or twice.

Divide between the prepared pans/tins and smooth the tops with a rubber spatula. Bake until a toothpick inserted in the center of each loaf comes out clean, about 45 minutes. Transfer to wire racks/cake coolers to cool slightly, then unmold onto the racks/coolers to cool completely. Use now, or wrap in plastic wrap and store at room temperature for up to 1 day. Wrap the other loaf in plastic wrap, place in a resealable plastic bag, and freeze for up to 3 months.

For the custard: Pour the milk into a medium saucepan and scrape in the vanilla seeds. Add the bean/pod halves and cook over medium heat until bubbles form around the edges of the pan. Remove from heat.

In a stand mixer, beat the egg yolks and sugar on medium-high speed until thick, about 5 minutes. With the mixer on low speed, sprinkle in the cornstarch/cornflour and beat until combined; stop the mixer and scrape down the sides of the bowl.

Strain the milk mixture. On low speed, add one ladleful milk mixture to the egg yolk mixture to temper. Continue, adding one ladleful at a time, until blended. Return to the saucepan and cook over low heat, stirring constantly,

until the custard coats the back of a spoon, 5 to 7 minutes; do not boil.

Strain the mixture through a fine-mesh sieve into a large bowl. Press plastic wrap directly on the surface of the custard and let cool; refrigerate for at least 2 hours or up to 1 day.

For the cranberries: In a medium saucepan, combine the cranberries, sugar, tangerine zest, juice, and ginger. Bring to a boil over medium-high heat. Reduce heat to medium-low and simmer for 10 to 15 minutes, or until the cranberries have popped and are softened. Remove from heat and let cool completely. Use now, or cover and refrigerate for up to 2 days.

For the whipped cream: Using an electric mixer or a whisk, beat the cream, sugar, and Grand Marnier until soft peaks form, about 5 minutes. Use now, or cover and refrigerate for up to 2 hours.

Cut the pumpkin bread into ½-in/12-mm slices. Place a layer of bread slices in the bottom of a trifle or other deep glass bowl, cutting the pieces to fit. Evenly spoon gingered cranberries over the slices. Add a layer of vanilla custard. Repeat the layers of pumpkin bread, cranberries, and vanilla custard, ending with the custard. You should have four or five layers, depending on the width of the bowl you're using. Spread the whipped cream over the top of the trifle and dust with ground cloves. Spoon onto plates and serve. The trifle can be made several hours ahead, without the whipped cream garnish, and stored in the refrigerator. Just before serving, add the whipped cream and dust with ground cloves.

What are biodynamic wines?

Biodynamic wines are those made using the biodynamic viticulture methods that originated with Rudolph Steiner (1861–1925) and predate the organic movement. Biodynamics integrates the ecological, the energetic, and the spiritual in viticulture. It extols the virtues of a self-sustained closed circle within the vineyard, providing rich habitat for animals and insects as well as plant life. Proponents of biodynamic farming claim increased health of the vineyards, and more vibrant aromas and flavors in the wines.

Like organic farming, biodynamic farming eschews chemical fertilizers, fungicides, and insecticides. It uses cover crops, green manures, and crop rotations to facilitate healthy growth. Biodynamics differs from organic farming in its beliefs in certain folk traditions, such as that the position of the moon and stars influences growth. Vines are planted only at certain phases of the moon, for example. The sun and light are key components in this system of viticulture, and vines are sprayed with ground quartz to enhance light and warmth. And in one of the more unusual biodynamic practices, cow manure is buried in cow horns over the winter, and the vineyard is sprayed with water mixed with this substance in the springtime.

Proponents of biodynamic viticulture are found in every winemaking country of the world, including Michel Chapoutier in France, and the Benziger family here in Sonoma. Hanna Winery follows some biodynamic practices: rather than using chemical fertilizers, for example, we grow cover crops and use compost. We minimize herbicides by hand hoeing weeds instead. But while biodynamics is fascinating, for now we'll leave the quartz crystals and buried cow manure to other vintners.

Holiday Open House

○ ○ ○

We have a grand tradition of holiday open houses here in the valley. They're a great way to entertain for a crowd.

Everything on this menu is intended to be served at room temperature, except for the soup, which is kept simmering on the stove for guests to help themselves to when they come in from the cold.

In general, the recipes serve 12 and can easily be multiplied. The ham will serve at least 20 for a buffet, and the wild rice salad can be doubled or tripled depending on the number of guests. The cookies can be made in multiple batches.

I set up a bar right near the front door for my guests, with sparkling water, white wine, and red wine; people are happy to help themselves. With this menu, I would choose a smooth Chardonnay to pair with the velvety cauliflower soup and the buttery tart. A Russian River Valley Pinot Noir would work nicely with the ham and the wild rice salad. Keep a pot of strong coffee on hand for the drivers, next to the platters of cookies.

Sicilian Tart with Chard, Feta, Pine Nuts, and Currants || SERVES 12 AS A BUFFET COURSE, OR 8 AS A FIRST COURSE

My husband and I took a trip to Sicily when I was seven months pregnant. The Sicilians love pregnant women, so I got extra helpings of pasta and gelato everywhere I went! For four hundred years, Sicily was ruled by the Arabs, so their cuisine melds traditional Italian flavors with Eastern Mediterranean influences. This savory tart is layered with the flavors of Sicily, and it tastes great at room temperature.

Chardonnay is a perfect accompaniment.

PASTRY DOUGH

1¼ cups/160 g all-purpose/plain flour

¼ tsp salt

7 tbsp/100 g cold unsalted butter, cut into chunks

3 tbsp ice water

FILLING

¼ cup/30 g pine nuts

2 tbsp extra-virgin olive oil

2 shallots, finely chopped

2 tbsp dried currants

1 lb/455 g Swiss chard, stemmed and chopped

1 tsp salt

½ tsp freshly ground pepper

1 cup/225 g fresh whole-milk ricotta cheese, drained

½ cup/70 g crumbled feta cheese

For the dough: In a food processor, pulse the flour and salt to blend. Add the butter and pulse until the mixture resembles pebbles. Add the ice water, 1 tbsp at a time, and pulse until the mixture just comes together. Turn onto a floured surface and shape into a disk. Wrap in plastic and refrigerate for at least 1 hour or up to 2 days.

Adjust an oven rack in the center of the oven. Preheat the oven to 375°F/190°C/ gas 5. On a floured surface, roll the dough into a 12-in/30.5-cm round. Fit the dough into a 10-in/25-cm round or square fluted tart pan/flan tin with a removable bottom, pushing the dough into the sides. Run the rolling pin over the top of the pan to trim the dough. Prick the dough all over with a fork. Fit a sheet of parchment/baking paper into the crust and add dried beans or pie weights. Bake for 30 minutes. Remove the paper and weights and bake for another 10 minutes, or until the crust is golden. Remove from the oven and let cool on a wire rack/cake cooler.

For the filling: Spread the pine nuts in a pie pan and toast in the hot oven for 10 minutes, or until golden. Pour into a bowl and let cool.

In a large, heavy saucepan, heat the olive oil over medium heat until shimmering. Add the shallots and sauté until translucent, about 3 minutes. Add the currants and toss to coat with the oil. Add the chard, cover, and cook for about 5 minutes, or until wilted. Add the salt and pepper. Transfer to a bowl and let cool. Drain the chard of any excess liquid.

Drain ricotta in a sieve lined with cheesecloth/muslin for 30 minutes before using; otherwise, the crust will be soggy. In a medium bowl, stir the ricotta and feta together until blended. Spread the cheese mixture evenly in the cooled crust. Layer the chard mixture over the top, then sprinkle the pine nuts evenly over the chard. When ready to serve, remove the sides of the tart pan and cut the tart into wedges.

Cream of Cauliflower and Fennel Soup

A hot soup is a wonderful way to welcome people into a wintertime gathering. I stack porcelain cups on the counter by the stove and let guests help themselves. This soup combines two vegetables that are at their best in winter, and its velvety texture is comforting on a cold night.

Cauliflower and cream call out for a rich Chardonnay.

2 tbsp unsalted butter

1 small onion, finely chopped

1 fennel bulb, trimmed, cored, and cut into 2-in/5-cm dice

1 large cauliflower, cored and coarsely chopped

1 cup/240 ml good-quality chicken stock

½ cup/120 ml heavy/double cream

Salt and freshly ground pepper

2 tbsp finely chopped fresh chives for garnish

In a medium soup pot, melt the butter over medium heat just until foaming. Add the onion and sauté until translucent, about 3 minutes. Add the fennel and toss to coat. Reduce heat to medium-low, cover, and cook until tender, about 10 minutes; do not brown. Add the cauliflower and toss to coat. Add the chicken stock, cover, and simmer until the cauliflower is tender, about 10 minutes.

Puree the soup in a blender or food processor, in batches if necessary, until smooth. Return to the pot. Whisk in the cream and salt and pepper to taste. Maintain at a low simmer over low heat, with a bowl of chives alongside for guests to add their own garnish.

Seeded Focaccia | SERVES 12 TO 14

This easy-to-make flat bread has a seeded, salty top, making it irresistible. The fennel seeds echo the anise flavor of the fennel in the soup. (I dare you to not eat the entire focaccia, especially if you serve it warm out of the oven.)

⅔ cup/165 ml plus 1 cup/240 ml warm (105° to 115°F/40° to 45°C) water

1 package (2¼ tsp) active dry yeast

½ cup/120 ml extra-virgin olive oil

5 cups/640 g all-purpose/plain flour

3½ tsp salt

1 tbsp fennel seeds

1 tbsp sesame seeds

1 tsp cumin seeds

Pour the ⅔ cup/165 ml warm water into a 4-cup/960-ml glass measure. Sprinkle the yeast over the water and stir until dissolved. Let stand for 5 minutes, or until foamy. Stir in the 1 cup/240 ml warm water and ¼ cup/60 ml of the olive oil.

In a food processor, pulse the flour and 2½ tsp of the salt to blend. With the machine running, gradually add the yeast mixture and process until the dough forms a sticky ball.

Turn out the dough on a floured surface and knead for 3 minutes, or until the dough is smooth and elastic. Form the dough into a ball and place in an oiled large bowl, turning the dough to coat it with oil. Cover with plastic wrap and place in a warm place to rise until doubled, about 1 hour.

Turn the dough out on the floured surface and roll it out into an 11-by-14-in/28-by-35.5-cm rectangle. Press the

dough into a baking sheet/tray or jelly-roll/Swiss roll pan of the same size. Cover completely with an oiled piece of plastic wrap and let rise until it reaches the top of the rim, about 1 hour.

Adjust an oven rack in the center of the oven. Preheat the oven to 425°F/220°C/gas 7. In a small, dry frying pan, stir the fennel, sesame, and cumin seeds over medium heat for 5 minutes, or until they release their fragrance. Do not let brown. Pour into a small bowl and stir in the remaining ¼ cup/60 ml olive oil.

Make indentations about ½ in/12 mm deep with your fingertips all over the dough. Brush the seeded oil mixture evenly over the dough. Sprinkle with the remaining 1 tsp salt and bake until golden, about 20 minutes. Remove from the oven and slide the focaccia out of the pan onto a wire rack/cake cooler to cool. Cut into squares to serve.

Quince-Glazed Ham with Mustard-Horseradish Sauce

SERVES 20 FOR A BUFFET PARTY, OR UP TO 16 FOR A DINNER

Here's the Future Farmers Fair pig again, this time as a holiday ham. Fresh ham has a much nicer texture than the smoked kind, almost like a pork loin.

There's nothing like a ham for a crowd. It's easy to cook, and it tastes great whether hot, warm, or cold. Quince jam and a lovely spicy-floral Gewürztraminer are used for the glaze, whose sweetness is countered with a tangy-hot sauce.

Serve the ham with the same Gewürztraminer used to make the glaze, or a lush Chardonnay or a Russian River Pinot Noir.

HAM AND GLAZE

1 cup/280 g quince jam

¼ cup/60 ml Dijon mustard

One 9-lb/4-kg bone-in ham/gammon, fat scored in a diamond pattern

1 bottle/750 ml Gewürztraminer

MUSTARD-HORSERADISH SAUCE

1 cup/240 ml crème fraîche

2 tbsp Dijon mustard

1 tbsp prepared horseradish

½ tsp salt

¼ tsp freshly ground pepper

For the ham and glaze: In a small saucepan, combine the quince jam and mustard. Whisk over medium heat until melted, about 2 minutes. Set aside to cool.

Preheat the oven to 325°F/165°C/gas 3. Place the ham/gammon, fat side up, on a rack placed in a roasting pan/tray. Pour the wine over the ham/gammon. Bake for 1 hour, basting every 20 minutes or so with the wine. At the end of the hour, brush the top and sides of the ham/gammon with the quince glaze. Bake for 40 minutes more, basting at the beginning and halfway through. Brush with the remaining glaze and bake for 20 minutes more, for a total baking time of 2 hours. Transfer the ham/gammon to a carving board, tent with aluminum foil, and let rest for 15 minutes. Strain the pan juices to serve with the ham/gammon, if desired.

For the mustard-horseradish sauce: In a small bowl, whisk together the crème fraîche, mustard, and horseradish. Season with the salt and pepper.

To serve, cut the ham/gammon into thin slices and serve at room temperature, with the sauce alongside, and the reserved pan juices, if you like.

Wild Rice Salad with Celery Root, Acorn Squash, and Leek

SERVES 12 FOR A BUFFET PARTY, OR 10 FOR A PLATED COURSE

We have a wine distributor from Minnesota who sends us a box of wild rice as a gift every Thanksgiving, and that was the inspiration for this recipe.

In this beautiful salad, the traditional mirepoix of celery, carrot, and onion is replaced by celery root, acorn squash, and leek. Visually dramatic, this dish is delicious at room temperature. Wild rice absorbs a tremendous amount of liquid, so you may need to add more water toward the end of the cooking process, depending on the size of the grain.

Serve this earthy, full-flavored salad with a Pinot Noir.

4 cups/960 ml chicken stock

2 cups/480 ml water

2 cups/430 g wild rice, rinsed and drained

2 tbsp extra-virgin olive oil

2 cups/280 g finely diced celery root

2 cups/280 g finely diced acorn squash

2 cups/230 g thinly sliced leek, white part only

2 tsp salt

1 tsp freshly ground pepper

VINAIGRETTE

¼ cup/60 ml extra-virgin olive oil

1 tbsp sherry vinegar

1 tsp balsamic vinegar

½ tsp salt

¼ tsp freshly ground pepper

In a large, heavy saucepan, bring the stock and water to a boil. Add the rice and reduce heat to low. Cover and simmer until the liquid is absorbed and the rice is tender, about 1 hour, adding more water if necessary toward the end of cooking. Remove from heat and pour the rice into a large bowl.

In a large sauté pan, heat the olive oil over medium heat until shimmering. Add the celery root, squash, leek, salt, and pepper and sauté for 3 minutes. Cover and cook over medium heat for 5 minutes more, or until the vegetables are tender.

For the vinaigrette: In a small bowl, whisk together the olive oil, vinegars, salt, and pepper.

Add the vegetable mixture to the rice and toss with the vinaigrette. Serve at room temperature.

Puntarelle and Satsuma Salad

Puntarelle is a Roman variety of chicory. Its leaves are light green and swordlike, with serrated edges. Like most chicories, it has a slightly bitter taste, which complements the honeyed sweetness of the Satsuma tangerines. Satsumas are prized here in Sonoma County, and the local chefs use them on their menus all winter long. Their skin is rough and mottled and their shape irregular, but their flavor makes up for their lack of beauty. Feel free to substitute other tangerines if you can't find Satsumas. The honey in the vinaigrette echoes the sweet tangerine flavor.

3 small Satsuma or other tangerines

¼ cup/60 ml extra-virgin olive oil

4 tsp white wine vinegar

2 tsp honey

2 tsp Dijon mustard

1 tsp salt

½ tsp freshly ground pepper

Leaves from 2 heads puntarelle chicory, or any other winter salad green, torn

Remove peel and pith from the tangerines with a knife, then cut the segments between the membranes. Reserve any juice for the vinaigrette. Set aside.

In a small bowl, whisk together the olive oil, vinegar, honey, mustard, salt, pepper, and any reserved tangerine juice.

In a salad bowl, toss the greens with the vinaigrette until well coated. Add the tangerine segments and toss gently to combine.

Allspice, Date, and Walnut Bars || MAKES 24 BARS

These bars remind me of the honey-laden Middle Eastern sweets my grandmother used to make. Exotic and familiar at the same time, the allspice-scented shortbread is topped with dates and crunchy walnuts.

2 cups/255 g all-purpose/plain flour

½ tsp salt

2 tsp ground allspice

¾ cup/170 g cold unsalted butter, cut into 1-in/2.5-cm chunks

½ cup/100 g packed brown sugar/ Demerara sugar

½ tsp vanilla extract/essence

2 cups/340 g chopped dates

2 cups/480 ml water

⅓ cup/75 ml honey

2 cups/225 g chopped walnuts

½ tsp grated orange zest

Adjust an oven rack in the center of the oven. Preheat the oven to 350°F/180°C/gas 4. In a food processor, pulse the flour, salt, and allspice until combined. Add the butter, brown sugar/Demerara sugar, and vanilla and pulse until the mixture looks sandy. Do not overwork; it will not form into dough. Pour into an ungreased 9-by-13-in/23-by-33-cm baking pan, using a metal spatula and your fingers to press it down. Bake for 20 minutes, or until lightly golden.

Meanwhile, in a medium saucepan, simmer the dates, water, and honey over low heat until thickened, about 10 minutes. Add the walnuts and orange zest and toss to coat. Spread the date mixture over the shortbread and bake for another 20 minutes. Transfer to a wire rack/cake cooler and let cool completely in the pan. Cut into 24 bars to serve.

Chocolate-Dipped Macaroons ‖ MAKES 36 COOKIES

Who doesn't love a macaroon? And anything chocolate dipped is just fine by me. My kids love to help me with the chocolate dipping, and soon we're all covered in chocolate. For a bit more sophistication, I use bittersweet chocolate instead of semisweet or milk.

2 large egg whites

Pinch of salt

One 14-oz/400-g package sweetened shredded/desiccated coconut

1 tsp almond extract/essence

One 14-oz/420-ml can sweetened condensed milk

12 oz/340 g best-quality bittersweet chocolate, chopped

Adjust an oven rack in the center of the oven. Preheat the oven to 325°F/165°C/gas 3. Line 2 baking sheet/trays with parchment/baking paper.

Using an electric mixer, beat the egg whites and salt until stiff, glossy peaks form. In a large bowl, combine the coconut, almond extract/essence, and condensed milk. Stir to blend. Carefully fold in the beaten egg whites.

Drop by rounded teaspoons onto the prepared pans. Bake for 20 minutes, or until golden brown. Transfer the cookies from the baking pans to wire racks/cake coolers and let cool.

In a double boiler over barely simmering water, melt the chocolate. Whisk until smooth and remove from heat. Dip each macaroon halfway into the melted chocolate and place on a parchment/baking paper–lined baking sheet/tray to set the chocolate.

American Viticultural Area (AVA): A known boundary that shares distinctive climates, soils, elevations, and physical features.

Appellation: A geographical area where grapes are grown and wines are produced.

Biodynamic winemaking: A method of winemaking that employs organic agriculture, emphasizes the holistic health of the soil, and uses a lunar planting calendar.

Bordeaux blend: A wine made from more than one of the five grape varieties indigenous to Bordeaux: Cabernet Sauvignon, Merlot, Cabernet Franc, Malbec, and Petit Verdot.

Brix: A measurement of the sugar content in grapes; named after the nineteenth-century German chemist A. F. W. Brix.

Brut: Denotes very dry Champagne.

Cabernet Franc: One of the lesser-known red grape varieties indigenous to Bordeaux; though primarily used as a blending grape, it is sometimes bottled as a varietal.

Cabernet Sauvignon: A red grape variety indigenous to France's Bordeaux region and planted widely in Napa and Sonoma Counties, Washington state, and Chile.

Carneros: A wine-growing region in the Sonoma and Napa Counties of California, north of San Pablo Bay.

Cava: Sparkling wine from Spain.

Champagne: Sparkling wine made using the *methode champenoise,* in the Champagne region in France.

Chardonnay: A white grape variety indigenous to France's Burgundy region and widely planted in California and most other wine regions of the world.

Chenin Blanc: A white wine variety indigenous to the Loire Valley in France, used to make both sparkling and still wines.

Cremant: Sparkling wine made from Chenin Blanc, from the Loire region of France.

Delicata: A variety of winter squash.

Farro: An ancient wheat similar to spelt.

Fumé Blanc: A wine variety made from Sauvignon Blanc, and usually aged in oak barrels.

Gewürztraminer: A white grape widely planted in Alsace, but also grown in California; it has a floral, spicy aroma and flavor.

Grenache: A red grape variety grown most widely in southern France and Spain. It is low in tannin and acidity and has juicy berry-like flavors. Grenache is usually blended with other varieties like Syrah to make Chateauneuf du Pape and Rose.

Kabocha: A variety of winter squash.

Kadota: A variety of green fig with rose-colored flesh.

Lolla Rossa: A variety of red-leaf lettuce.

Merlot: A red grape indigenous to the Bordeaux region of France and widely planted in California, Washington state, Australia, and Chile.

Methode champenoise: A method of making sparkling wine that includes a primary fermentation as well as a secondary fermentation that occurs when sugar and yeast are added to the tank and the wine is bottled. The wine is aged on the yeast lees, then the yeast sediment is disgorged. After disgorging, the dosage (a mixture of cane sugar, wine, and Cognac or brandy), is added to adjust tartness. The wine is aged for a few months in the bottle, then released. Any wine designated Champagne on its label must use this method.

Meursault: An appellation in France's Burgundy region, near Beaune. Meursault produces mainly white wines from Chardonnay grapes, with a distinctive minerality.

Moscato: Dessert wine made from the Muscat grape.

Muhammarah: A Middle Eastern dip made with red peppers, walnuts, and pomegranate molasses.

Orrechiette: Pasta formed in the shape of little ears.

Pinot Blanc: A white wine grape variety that's a genetic mutation of Pinot Gris.

Pinot Gris: A white wine grape variety with bluish-gray fruit. In Italy, it is known as Pinot Grigio.

Pinot Meunier: A red grape variety primarily used in the production of Champagne and sparkling wine. It ripens earlier than Pinot Noir, and contributes fruity flavors and aromas. Pinot Meunier is sometimes used to make light-bodied still wine or Rosé.

Pinot Noir: A red wine grape variety grown widely in France's Burgundy region, and in Oregon and California.

Prosecco: Sparkling wine from Italy.

Puntarelle: Roman chicory.

Ramps: Wild onions; also known as wild leeks.

Refractometer: An instrument used to measure sugar content in grapes using degrees Brix.

Riesling: A white wine grape variety indigenous to the Rhine region of Germany. Noteworthy dry Rieslings are made in Alsace, Australia, and California.

Rosé: A pink wine made of red grapes that have been allowed to stay on the skins for a short time.

Sangiovese: An Italian red grape variety mainly used to make Chianti. California winemakers are experimenting with it as a varietal.

Satsuma: A variety of tangerine.

Sauternes: A dessert wine from the Bordeaux region of France, primarily made with Sauvignon Blanc and Semillon.

Sauvignon Blanc: A grape variety grown widely in France, California, and New Zealand.

Semolina: A yellow flour made from durum wheat.

Shiraz: The Australian name for a red wine made from the Shiraz grape; both the wine and the grape are known elsewhere as Syrah.

Sommelier: A trained and knowledgeable wine professional.

Sorrel: A perennial herb with swordlike leaves and a lemony flavor.

Steelhead: An ocean-going trout with flesh similar in color to that of wild salmon.

Sulfites (sulfur dioxide): A preservative and antioxidant widely used to preserve wine.

Sur lies: A method of aging wine on the yeast lees.

Syrah: A red grape variety thought to have originated in Persia. Syrah is widely planted in the Rhône Valley of France, in Australia (where it is called Shiraz), and in California.

Tahini: Sesame paste; used in Middle Eastern cuisine.

Tempranillo: A red grape indigenous to Spain's Rioja region.

Trichloranisole (TCA): A chemical compound that infects a wine cork with mold that smells like musty cardboard.

Varietal: A wine made primarily from a single grape variety. In California, a wine must contain 75 percent of a single varietal in order to be labeled with the name of that particular grape variety.

Viognier: A white grape with a floral aroma, indigenous to the Rhône Valley of France.

Yeast lees: Deposits of residual yeast left at the bottom of a wine barrel or tank after fermentation. Wines aged on the lees (a process known as *sur lies*) have a distinctive yeasty aroma and flavor.

Zinfandel: A red grape variety grown widely in California; it is indigenous to Croatia and related to the Primitivo grape in Italy.

INDEX